Praise for *Sa...*

A *New York Times Book Re...*

"[Emily Rapp Black] movingly recounts her struggle to live fully without forgetting." —*People*

"Black's power as a writer means she can take us with her to places that normally our minds would refuse to go. . . . [An] often beautiful jewel of a book." —*The New York Times Book Review*

"There's a swagger to Black's prose." —*Los Angeles Times*

"In *Sanctuary*, [Rapp Black] writes . . . with elegant poise and a tenderness that is equal parts raw and generous. . . . She writes with fierce honesty and zero sentimentality, in a way that distinguishes her from many others who write about grief and trauma. . . . Rapp Black's exquisite prose is as compelling as her intellectual rigor. . . . In the end, *Sanctuary* is not a memoir of grief or of survival, but rather simply a story about living. Rapp Black is astute and sensitive, and she invites readers to bear witness to the intimate, intense, and profound experiences of losing and gaining so much. . . . Having taken the journey, she invites us along and, in doing so, opens our world to new possibilities." —*Los Angeles Review of Books*

"A celebration of love, and life . . . as well as an investigation of what it means to be human . . . Black's voice is singularly lyrical, singularly bracing. She is obsessed with the potency of language, offering favorite phrases and lines, sometimes contextualizing but more often quoting with the confidence of a reader who has made the sentences her own." —*Alta Journal*

"A raw, vulnerable examination of resilience and living with both loss and joy." —*Working Mother*

"This open and frank reflection centers on what it means to be resilient. . . . A must for fans of Rapp's previous memoirs and for any reader trying to better understand grief and trauma." —*Library Journal*

"Rapp Black . . . shines in this stirring account of life after the death of her son Ronan. . . . Rapp Black asserts that, in life, resilience requires no extraordinary measures because life itself—with its inevitable losses—demands resilience for survival. The prose is lyrical and hypnotic but never overwrought or contrived. This is a mesmerizing and unforgettable tale." —*Publishers Weekly*

"A meticulous examination of the aftershocks of the loss of a child . . . a searing, uncompromising effort to wrestle with permanent grief." —*Kirkus Reviews*

"In this probing memoir, [Emily Rapp Black] shares her journey as a mother split in two by the painful past and the joyful present. . . . Rejecting the characterizations of those who tell her she's resilient or who compare her to a mythic phoenix, rising from the ashes, she struggles to a more human-sized answer—people do what they must do—and a more nuanced definition of resilience. . . . Comfort comes from her wisdom in perceiving that all the people who came before us—now unseen but with us still—hold us up, supporting us in all that we do." —*Booklist*

"A book of rare power and grace . . . Reading this extraordinarily thoughtful writer and her luminous prose was, for me, sanctuary."
—Will Schwalbe, *New York Times* bestselling author of *The End of Your Life Book Club*

"In these pages, Emily Rapp Black excavates the meaning of resilience, putting aside brittle clichés about heroism and strength to uncover a richer, messier, more beautiful picture of what it means to live amidst both love and loss. This is a lyrical, deep, funny, eyes-wide-open, ultimately comforting book. I adored it, and—if you are searching for how to live in a broken world—so will you."
—Lucy Kalanithi

"*Sanctuary* opens up the space between life and death in order to show us how love gets born over and over again—a fierce and unflinching love, a love that has to travel trauma and truth to evolve. Rapp Black's book is a precise and complex articulation of a journey that has nothing to do with the puny hero's journey. It's bigger than that. It's the story of the relationship between creation and decreation as it lives in the bodies of women. This book

will give us better ways to tell the stories of motherhood, desire, despair, resistance, and resilience. This book will change lives."
—Lidia Yuknavitch, author of *The Book of Joan* and *The Small Backs of Children*

"Every once in a while, a book comes along that ushers us to the very center of a profound truth that we don't so much learn, as recognize. Emily Rapp Black takes us there in *Sanctuary*, reminding us in achingly beautiful prose that pain and pleasure, grief and aliveness, exist not apart but together in the dark matter, the liminal space we occupy when we do what the living do: we love, we love, we love."
—Dani Shapiro, *New York Times* bestselling author of *Inheritance*

"Have you ever wished for a light to guide you when life asks you to bear what you think you cannot bear? Emily Rapp Black is that light; *Sanctuary* is that guide. There's no handbook for loss, but there are these pages and Rapp Black's beautiful, breathtaking language that lifts and rises. I've thrown books about grief across the room in rage at their uselessness. Not this book. It will carry you. Rapp Black has again opened the door to her generous heart and let us in—and what beats there is holy and fierce and lifegiving."
—Sarah Sentilles, author of *Draw Your Weapons*

"*Sanctuary* is an absolute marvel—gorgeous and bold, astonishing in insight and unsparing in candor. With aching vulnerability and compassion, Emily Rapp Black maps the topography of heartrending loss and erects upon it a refuge of otherworldly resilience. As a writer, a mother, and a woman, Rapp Black is a profound inspiration—not because she's fearless but because she's courageous. To understand the distinction, read this beautiful book."
—Bret Anthony Johnston, author of *Remember Me Like This*

"Not since *When Breath Becomes Air* has a memoir conveyed such profound loss alongside such luminous and life-affirming love. With exquisitely precise prose, Emily Rapp Black describes what it is like to mother a dead boy and an alive girl simultaneously: being pulled in both directions, juggling sorrow and guilt, but moving toward light and life. *Sanctuary* broke my heart and mended it, expanding it through truth and beauty."
—Adrienne Brodeur, author of *Wild Game*

Sanctuary

Sanctuary

a memoir

Emily Rapp Black

RANDOM HOUSE

New York

Published in the United States by Random House, an imprint and division of Penguin Random House LLC, New York.

RANDOM HOUSE and the HOUSE colophon are registered trademarks of Penguin Random House LLC.

Originally published in hardcover in the United States by Random House, an imprint and division of Penguin Random House LLC, in 2021.

Grateful acknowledgment is made to the following for permission to reprint previously published material:

Copper Canyon Press c/o The Permissions Company, LLC: "Spring," "Death of a Child, Part 1," and excerpts from "Origins of Violence," "Winter Variations," and "Influence" from *The Dream of Reason*, copyright © 2018 by Jenny George. Reprinted by permission of The Permissions Company, LLC on behalf of Copper Canyon Press, coppercanyonpress.org.
Graywolf Press c/o The Permissions Company, LLC: "Earth" ["If you respect . . ."] from *Colosseum* by Katie Ford, copyright © 2008 by Katie Ford; excerpts from "The Fire" and "Song After Sadness" from *Blood Lyrics* by Katie Ford, copyright © 2014 by Katie Ford; excerpt from "A Walk Around the Property" from *Priest Turned Therapist Treats Fear of God* by Tony Hoagland, copyright © 2018 by Tony Hoagland; excerpt from "After a Death" translated by Robert Bly from *The Half-Finished Heaven: The Best Poems of Tomas Tranströmer*, copyright © 2001 by Tomas Tranströmer, translation copyright © 2001 by Robert Bly. All poetry reprinted by permission of The Permissions Company on behalf of Graywolf Press, Minneapolis, Minnesota, graywolfpress.org.
HarperCollins Publishers: "The Wild Iris" from *The Wild Iris* by Louise Glück, copyright © 1992 by Louise Glück. Used by permission of HarperCollins Publishers.
Tupelo Press c/o The Permissions Company, LLC: Excerpts from "Heart," "What I Carried," and "Rough Air" from *Good Bones* by Maggie Smith, copyright © 2017 by Maggie Smith. Reprinted by permission of The Permissions Company, LLC on behalf of Tupelo Press, tupelopress.org.

LIBRARY OF CONGRESS CATALOGING-IN-PUBLICATION DATA
Names: Rapp Black, Emily, author.
Title: Sanctuary: a memoir / Emily Rapp Black.
Description: First edition. | New York: Random House, [2021]
Identifiers: LCCN 2020014287 (print) | LCCN 2020014288 (ebook) | ISBN 9780525510963 (trade paper) | ISBN 9780525510956 (ebook)
Subjects: LCSH: Rapp Black, Emily. | Parents of terminally ill children—Biography. | Resilience (Personality trait)
Classification: LCC BF698.35.R47 R36 2021 (print) | LCC BF698.35.R47 (ebook) | DDC 818/.603 [B]—dc23
LC record available at https://lccn.loc.gov/2020014287
LC ebook record available at https://lccn.loc.gov/2020014288

Printed in the United States of America on acid-free paper

randomhousebooks.com

9 8 7 6 5 4 3 2 1

Book design by Debbie Glasserman

FOR CHARLIE AND KB

Sanctuary

The Bridge, 2012

You may do this, I tell you, it is permitted.
Begin again the story of your life.

JANE HIRSHFIELD, FROM "DA CAPO"

I leaned against the guardrail above the Rio Grande Gorge Bridge in New Mexico, 565 feet above the river below, my heart beating fire. Heat swelled in my chest. A cold spring of intention lay coiled in my belly.

Under the July sun the high desert of New Mexico swept out in every direction, flush with the horizon, stark and beige with an occasional swipe of green, the line between heaven and earth impossible to distinguish. Scattered under such a sky, the sand- and earth-colored adobe buildings in the small town of Taos resembled broken pottery pieces—shattered, accidental, lost. The air at this altitude was thin and dusty; the sun against the skin intense and direct, able to scorch in a flash. Tourists and visitors strolled by, chatting and laughing, wearing visors and sandals, their shoulders striped with sunburn. Along the concrete footpath that ran the length of the bridge, roadside vendors sat behind handwritten signs advertising INDIAN JEWELRY AUTHENTIC, the rounded stones in the rings and bracelets and earrings blinking as clear and blue as the sky above us. The clouds looked deliberately arranged: fluffy as a dream, airy as balloons, moving languidly as if straight from a picture postcard. I found this stark and relentless beauty absurd—even grotesque. The rich white tourists surveyed the goods made by the native people of this land—assessing, deciding.

I leaned in a bit more and pressed my C-section scar, finally after two years gone white and numb, against the barrier, a white metal fence bearing a few names scribbled in pen—AARON LOVES IRIS—signs of those who once stood along this massive rift across the otherwise flat lands between Carson National Forest and the Sangre de Cristo Mountains.

That morning, I had finished teaching a master class in nonfiction at the writers' workshop in Taos, considered my one-on-one student meetings scheduled for late afternoon, and realized I had plenty of time. I told my parents I needed to take a walk, get some coffee, get "off campus," and they easily agreed to care for my son, Ronan, while I was away. They had been caring for him while I taught, talked with students, listened, and tried to help people order the chaos of their lives through storytelling. I kissed Ronan's face, hugged his still, soft body, looked into his green-gold eyes, which only ever saw me partially and now saw nothing at all, got in my car, and thought, *Now is as good a time as any*. I had been to the bridge only once before, with Ronan secured in the front carrier, his sleeping body still and warm against my chest.

Peering into the cavernous gorge was like encountering the impact of long-ago violence, perhaps a prehistoric stomp from the gigantic foot of an angry, mythical animal on a murderous cross-country trek. Feeling like a witness to some great destruction appealed to me. I stretched my arms farther and let them dangle, helped by gravity, until my fingertips began to tingle, and until the noise and chatter of people walking past began to dissipate and then disappear. I was lost in the promise of this emptiness, the sound of it, which was the absence of sound apart from a small rock loosening from the steep bank to tumble into the dry brush, rolling down down down until it disappeared from view. I closed my eyes and heard *whomp whomp whomp* like an invitation: *Yes. Jump. Do it.* The space below was hollow, magnetic, literally an opening. A mouth to fall into, as deep as any desire.

This particular summer of my thirty-eighth year was marked by the greatest suffering I had known, a rupture that a crater of any size in any ground and beneath any sky failed to accurately depict: a sick and dying child: my son, Ronan; a faltering marriage, which was turning cruel and wouldn't survive the bludgeon of our son's medieval, incurable illness; conversations that ended in *you make me sick, I can't fucking stand to look at you, get out of my sight;* a heart so saturated with dread it was physical work to bear it; a mind so fractured I rushed to make sense of my unpredictable thoughts at every turn. My mind was shifting and molting as my life broke slowly apart, like some strange and painful rebirth, but with no imaginable future—for what mother can imagine a future without her child? How would I spend my days? What, quite literally, would I do with myself? The world felt as harrowing and gaping as the hole in the ground I stood above, hovering like a fearful, angry bird.

Every part of the life I had known—practical and emotional—was disappearing, collapsing, burning to the ground. My life was in free fall, the world smoldered, and I was barely catching my breath in the smoke of each long day turning into the next. At night I tapped a handful of Xanax into my palm, then forced myself to return all but one pill to the bottle. I had been given the unspeakable responsibility of seeing my son through to his death, and yet all I had been able to do was write about it, think about it. Beyond that? I had no idea. For the first time, my imagination—the source of solace and comfort, of inspiration and relief that had sustained me all my life up to this point—was failing me. Without it, I was entirely unmoored. I stood on that bridge and felt completely lost. Here, perhaps, was a solution. Nobody took much notice of me; plenty of people were leaning over the metal rail, testing their limits, closing their eyes, straightening up and exclaiming, "Whoa. Dizzy!" Or stating the obvious: "It sure is a long way down!"

While Ronan's life was "unraveling," as the hospice team described it, a word intended to be less startling than "ending," I'd been flirting with erratic behavior, the life I had built around my son and his father unraveling as well. I slept with men I hardly knew yet tried to impress, as if trying on a new skin for a week, a night, or a moment might offer temporary relief. As if convincing someone to love me would make me feel worthy of love, instead of like a worthless mother who could do nothing to protect her child. I'd driven drunk through falling snow, weeping, my hands trembling on the wheel; I'd pulled people to me in nightclubs, at bars, and then just as easily let them go. I'd wake up in a strange man's bed in the middle of the night, or sometimes with a woman, and I'd feel the urge to write. Sometimes I'd realize after I'd skulked out the door that I'd forgotten my keys, so I'd sneak back in like a burglar, tiptoeing over a drum set, a baseball glove, a pile of dirty clothes that I didn't recognize and would never see again.

When I knew my marriage was over in all but legal name, I spent a night with a man I had long desired in a ratty hotel in Brooklyn where the bedsheets were made of paper and there were no locks on the doors. Before we stumbled into this cheap and smelly room, we'd been walking along Christopher Street, leaves crunching beneath our feet, wildly drunk, making out on corners for minutes at a time as if we were madly in love (perhaps in that moment we were), or newly married, and all the while I knew that I would never go back to Ronan's father because I didn't love him anymore and struggled to remember a time when I did. As I inhaled this man's odor and felt his strong, young hands on my back, against my face, I wondered if I did actually love him, or if maybe I had never loved anyone and never would.

Later, as we rolled around on the thin excuse for a mattress in our by-the-hour digs, I asked this man, "What do you want to do? I'll do anything," and that was true: yes, I was so unhinged by desire, aching with it, and I vividly remember how it felt to be pressed next to him, already memorizing the shape of his shoulders, aware of the warmth of his hands.

How the feeling of being wanted was so similar to feeling alive. I was ready and willing to shed any part of myself if it meant even a touch of relief.

Deliberately gaining and losing connections, if that's what these were, felt like training for some truly transformative event, which I was. But how does one prepare to witness her child's death?

I wanted to save what could not be saved, and that was Ronan, my *boy,* but he was leaving the world no matter what; dying no matter what.

"Promise me you won't kill yourself," my best friend, Emily, implored when I called her in London only moments after receiving Ronan's terminal diagnosis in January 2011, as if she understood where my mind would immediately go. I had promised her, again and again; and my parents, too, who were terrified by my behavior and would be devastated if I chose to take my life; but on that day in Taos I thought, *I'm sorry, Em; I'm sorry, Mom and Dad. I'm sorry, Ronan. I failed you, but I'm done.* I felt ready to break any pact with every person, with myself, and especially with the world. I had traveled to this bridge gripped with a sudden, singular purpose, an arrow searching for its mark.

Sweat tunneled down my back and along the sides of my waist; my thighs shook a bit and then went numb. I stretched the length of my upper body out even farther over the rail's edge. My neck began to feel weightless, as if it might easily lift from my spine. I heard passersby slow their footsteps and then keep walking. All along the bridge people hung over the bar to take pictures of their sandaled feet or a faraway rafter headed to the famous Taos "box" of white water, the boat just a tiny, trembling smudge from this distance. *Do it. End this. Can you do it?* A voice from somewhere—mine, perhaps not mine. And then I straightened up and stepped back. I could not do it.

I cannot say for certain what held me back: it wasn't faith, it wasn't God, it wasn't grit or determination or hope or the "bravery" and "strength" with which I was often labeled, and it wasn't fear. I was not afraid to die; death would offer relief from watching my son die, his tiny, helpless body racked by an illness that was slowly rotting his brain: a slow death—from the inside out—as every complicated physical and biological network that made life possible was ravaged and torched. From the moment of his birth, he never had a chance. Would I be a coward for leaving him? Perhaps, but it didn't reduce the desire to be free of the slow agony of losing him; it didn't lessen my dread of living without him.

I couldn't leap. I was stopped, in part, by two revelations that arrived simultaneously, like two parallel beams pressed one to each side of my body, as if I were lying, squeezed and supported, between them.

I can describe it like this: as teenagers in rural Nebraska, after keggers in the cornfields on the edges of our small town, my friends and I used to lie down between the train tracks and wait. We called it "riding the rails," as if we were a band of intrepid travelers instead of working-class kids who shopped at the same stores and had the same summer jobs and parroted one another's verbal expressions (*What a dweeb, That person is so LOW,* and other eighties insult gems). We were kids stuck in a flat town stuck in the middle of a flat state stuck in the middle of the country, the majority of it largely unknown to us except through library books and the news. Our vacations involved soft-sided campers and scummy motel pools, not sunny resorts. Nobody I knew had ever had a spa treatment.

As a teenager, I was the only person I'd ever known who lived with a "different" body, having had my leg amputated at the age of four as a result of a birth defect; my wooden leg was a part of me I fastidiously worked to avoid revealing, even to myself. I was living in a body I hated and deliberately starved; living with a mind that either couldn't quit or felt entirely empty; living in a world that felt small but also vast and unknowable and therefore dangerous.

On those sticky summer nights riding the rails, the world buzzed with insects and the anticipation only sheltered teenagers can feel on the outskirts of a nothing town. The earth was damp and smelled of fuel oil, a meaty, thick scent I've always loved. The sky was a black tarp uninterrupted by shadows or trees or bushes. Flat sky stretched over flat land. Lying on my back, hemmed in by the rails, felt like floating. I longed for a new place, a new sky, wished for different trees and new people and the noise of a city that was more than just the trumped-up cow town of Lincoln, our capital city. On nights like this, blinking into nothingness, I almost believed I might get out of the middle of this nowhere place and never return. Where would I go? Somewhere. I felt electric, electrified.

I was willing to wait a long time, stretched along those tracks, anticipating a train. I was always the winner. Most people jumped up as soon as the metal began to vibrate, suggesting an oncoming train, but there was something about the feeling of danger and fear that emboldened me, made me stay. I was taken with the idea of being the best, a competitive, striving nature that I would never fully leave behind and that would serve me until it did no longer. I waited until the final possible second; until I felt the air shift—a breeze across my face, at my neck, lifting my hair, then the low hoot of a faraway whistle growing closer and more earnest. My friends standing in the weeds shouted *"Rappstar!"* a high school nickname they painted on the side of the red 1978 Ford Fairmont my father gave me on my sixteenth birthday, a gas-guzzling raft of a car outfitted with an eight-track cassette player.

"You're scaring the shit out of us," they screamed, their voices panicked, and finally I joined them in the waist-high weeds, the pound of adrenaline and the humming in my body a welcome relief from the numbness and boredom and confusion and shame that punctuated those days.

Decades later, on this afternoon in the middle of my life, in the middle of this crucible of experience, this great maw of grief, standing in the middle of a bridge in a far different part of the world, one still defined by the vastness of the land, the bloom of endless sky, I thought:

I don't want to *live* my life, this life; I want my son's suffering to end, and my own, and for this unbearable waiting for death to simply stop.

I don't want to *end* my life, this life. I want to love again, to know hope and happiness, to be in the world, doing work that feels real and meaningful.

Both statements felt equally true, as if they were overlapping, like the ink that soaks through wet newsprint, leaving the letters to mingle and bleed together. It was not either/or; it was both/and. The two stories were the same story.

Or maybe what pulled me back from the edge of the bridge was another force entirely, and one that did not originate with me or within me but was part of my fabric as a living, breathing thing. The will to live; this insistence that every organism, no matter its sense of self or cognitive ability or intelligence or even brainpower, possesses for survival, even against remarkable odds. A body racked by disease will still fight for breath. People in life-threatening situations will do what they need to survive: cut off an arm, steal another's food, sleep with the enemy. A dying plant stretches its withered leaves toward the light. A tree heals its wounds, even if the scars that remain within the bark force it to create a new shape. A bug circling a sink's drain will go down fighting, a wing flapping like a transparent flag.

In "The Death of the Moth," an essay published in 1942, one year after her death by suicide, Virginia Woolf observes with tenderness as a moth fights to live within the parameters of possibilities he's been given:

He flew vigorously to one corner of his compartment, and, after waiting there a second, flew across to the other. What remained for him but to fly to a third corner and then to a fourth? That was all he could do, in spite of the size of the downs, the width of the sky, the far-off smoke of houses, and the romantic voice, now and then, of a steamer out at sea. What he could do he did. Watching him, it seemed as if a fibre, very thin but pure, of the enormous energy of the world had been thrust into his frail and diminutive body. As often as he crossed the pane, I could fancy that a thread of vital light became visible. He was little, or nothing, but life.

Simply put, we are engineered to live.

Inevitably, death wins, but not without the moth's instinctive fight to stay alive for as long as possible. Bugs might flail against a windowpane, but they're not melodramatic about it. What the moth could do while it was living, it did. What it could do to keep on living, it did, without thinking or railing or worrying or talking to a therapist or a friend or taking a pill or closing down a bar. The gift of life is instinctively understood as a gift, particularly when we are about to lose it, or when our most difficult experiences start to squeeze us tightly.

Even when it feels like the world is against us (and I felt that acutely during the crucible of that summer, which I knew would be Ronan's last), or unsafe for us; even when we move through deepening darkness, or a wilderness that becomes increasingly treacherous; even as we turn around and around, feeling lost and wretched, abandoned and alone, part of us, even the smallest part, maybe one we didn't know even existed until it was threatened, longs to be in the world. Not necessarily to have meaning and purpose, although that is certainly ideal, but to *be*, like Woolf's long-dead moth immortalized in countless anthologies taught in first-year English courses. We are hardwired to be tethered to the world and to fight for our place within it, to take up space, no matter the cost. Call it resilience, call it strength, call it biology.

Being granted a life comes with that innate sense that we are meant to live it, even on the days when any other option seems preferable.

Even Ronan, a boy without cognition, with no sense of self, with no physical ability to live or move or, in the end, to swallow, would fight to live in the final moments of his life. *What he could do he did.* But I would learn that later.

On this particular afternoon in the New Mexico desert that was for a few brief years my home, I straightened up, stepped away from the bridge, and walked back into my sad and wrenching life that was also—no doubt about it—full of wonder. The world felt like a miserable, unsafe place, but it was still the world I knew, and that knowledge felt like a close cousin of love.

> *I carried my fear of the world*
> *and my love for the world.*
> *I carried my terrible awe....*
> *I carried my fear of the world*
> *and it taught me how to carry it.*
> Maggie Smith, from "What I Carried"

The work ahead of me would be to find a way to live in the world—full of cruelty and beauty—that I clearly could not disavow. This, of course, is everybody's work, to live through suffering, to search out a safe resting place, the heart's sanctuary, although each of us is given a different task to manage—most often one we didn't ask for. The world doesn't care if you choose to stay alive, but it will hold you for as long as you are living. This indifference not only provides solace, I would later understand, but also is cause for celebration.

In one of the rural churches where my father served as a pastor, the first in my memory, I loved descending the stairs to join the Sunday potluck dinner in the basement. The smells of roast beef and sugary Swedish cookies and percolating coffee made my mouth water. I walked slowly to let my hunger and anticipation build, and also to have a long look at the banner hanging at the entrance to the fellowship hall. There, draped over a wooden dowel, written on a long piece of orange felt, was a message in green felt letters that were slightly uneven and clearly cut by hand: DON'T WALK IN FRONT OF ME, I MAY NOT FOLLOW. DON'T WALK BEHIND ME, I MAY NOT LEAD. WALK BESIDE ME, AND JUST BE MY FRIEND. A felt evergreen tree and a felt bee hovering over a felt daisy punctuated the sentences and the sentiment. Two people-shaped cutouts, holding felt hands, stood together in the corner.

The scene was truly pastoral and bucolic, the message a clear request that held within it a promise. Unlike some of the other banners hanging around the church—MAKE ME AN INSTRUMENT OF THY PEACE, and FORGIVE AS YOU WERE FORGIVEN—this particular directive seemed challenging but actually doable. Early in my life I understood the value of making—and cherishing—a friend. I loved being trusted and confided in, relished the delight and comfort that I found in friendship, and I quickly grew to rely on a network: I had playdates and then pen pals, and as a teenager and then young adult I was always on the phone or writing and receiving letters. Later I would fall from a great height into this web of women and men (some of whom I'd known since girlhood), and it would catch and hold me like a tender but unbreakable net.

I didn't have to kill that girl on the bridge. My trepidation and my sadness, lived out in the world, which I began to notice and experience in a new way, would teach me how to be a part of it again. "I carried my fear of the world/and it became my teacher" (Maggie Smith). I would befriend this girl, my parallel self: a loyal friend if I could acknowledge her, knowing that she would never leave me. Instead, she'd walk next to me—not in front, not behind, but beside, a witness keeping the story, keeping time, and keeping step with whatever came next, in the only world I'd been given or would ever know, living the only life I'd ever have to lead.

CHAPTER ONE

This Particular Fire

When a human is asked about a particular fire,
she comes close:
then it is too hot,
so she turns her face—

and that's when the forest of her bearable life appears,
always on the other side of the fire.

KATIE FORD, FROM "THE FIRE"

My three-year-old daughter, Charlie, screams for twenty uninterrupted minutes after I break her graham cracker at snack time. She asks instead for white rice, and it must be "ice cold," but the ice cubes used to chill it (a process she supervises) can no longer be present or even in view at the time of delivery in the bowl, which must be pink, and which she must select herself from the drawer where I keep her collection of plastic dishes. "I do it!" she insists, a statement she repeats countless times a day, often stomping a tiny foot and crossing her arms, like a parody of toddler behavior, only she is quite serious. I remind myself *she can do it; let her do it.* This, the teachers at her Montessori school have assured me, is the best way to foster independence, that essential building block of human development. "Development": a word that once made me hollow with sadness.

My experience caring for Ronan was so different, so quiet, all of the activity internal: the pain of watching him worsen and fade; the constant, wrenching speculation (Was he hurting? Was he worsening? Were we closer to the end, and what came after? Was that a seizure or just a hiccup or a giggle?), that I'm learning for the first time how to be a mother to a child who is independent and will continue to be so; a child who I hope will live a long life and attend my funeral and scatter my ashes in a place of her choosing, as is the right order of things, or at least the order we think we sign up for when or if we start families.

Ronan was my silent, sweet companion. Charlie talks back, has opinions, ideas, moods, and so many strongly felt emotions that she can express and sometimes name. "I feel lost," she tells me almost wistfully when she's confused, and sometimes, "I'm sad," when she gets pushed at school and she "pushed back so strong" but then clearly feels bad about her actions; or, in New York City, in a hotel room all to ourselves visiting friends, "This is so fun and I'm so happy!" In moments like these, the shift from one parenting experience to another is jarring; the adjustment knocks me off kilter, like a top spinning wildly on a table and falling to the floor, spinning still.

Charlie and I eat the rice and sing "Gorilla in the Sky" (original lyrics and three-line score by me) and then we're off to the grocery store, where I buy Charlie a twenty-dollar enormous princess castle Mylar balloon in exchange for the promise that she will *please stay buckled in the cart* for thirty minutes while I race through the aisles getting only half of what's on the list, in addition to much that's not on it: a massive cupcake topped with a fist of whipped cream and bright pink candy sprinkles; a box as big as a brick of Goldfish crackers; and bubble bath that makes popping noises as it dissolves in the water, creating a shade of blue that looks like toxic sludge. "I won't drink it!" she promises.

As soon as we arrive home and are headed up the back stairs, stopping to look at lizards, checking out the many birdhouses left in the yard by the previous owners, calling out for Meatball, the stray cat Charlie has named and who we sometimes see skulking through the yard, searching for the tuna and sardines we leave for him on a pink plastic plate, Charlie gets distracted and releases her balloon. "No, wait!" I shout, as if the balloon will mind me. I drop the grocery bags in an effort to save the shiny pink castle from floating up to the top of the tallest palm tree in our wild Southern California yard, where it rocks in the slight breeze, taunting Charlie, the four princesses—Ariel, Rapunzel, Jasmine, Cinderella—slowly rotating past her vision.

"Princesses, no!" Charlie cries, as if they have failed to invite her to the party in the tree. She turns to me. "*Why Why Why* can't you get it? You're tall! *Why?*" She stands on her tiptoes and reaches upward with her sticky, sweaty hands, sobbing. After fifteen minutes that feel like a hundred, I am able to coax her, sweating and sniffling and practically hyperventilating, off the porch, where the temperature hovers around 107 degrees. I collect the scattered groceries and pile them on the table, toss the raft of broken eggs in the trash, put the battered milk carton in the refrigerator, and return to a despondent little girl, sitting on the couch with her hands in her lap, silent and sad, floating in an existential, tear-swamped toddler daze. I try every distraction and consolation—songs about fairies, twinkling stars, and swimming turtles. I attempt to soothe with mom dream logic: "Maybe the balloon will float down again!" "Isn't it so fun to look at the princesses having a tea party high up in the trees?" "It's like a castle in the sky!" "How special and fun!"

Charlie anchors her head over my shoulder and sobs inconsolably.

If I were a member of any mothering blogs or groups, which I am not, I might start a post with a faux-exasperated "OMG" and title it "Life with a 'Threenager.'" I'm not in these groups because I worry that the "normal" concerns of this mother of Charlie, who is alive and thriving, will make me forget the mother of Ronan, who is gone (isn't she?), so I stay in the parenting online communities where I do feel at home and where I am a member: those populated by women whose children have died, primarily from Tay-Sachs or similar diseases, but the club remains open to any parent who has experienced this particular life-splitting, identity-shifting, world-defining loss. These mothers post updates like *When he's really sad, my husband starts building fences. He's out there for hours, pounding posts into the ground. The thing is, we don't need any more fences;* or this: *I feel like sadness is rotting me from the inside out.* Crisis makes sense to me, but not the kind that many people experience with their children: broken arms, broken hearts, a bad grade on a test, a high fever that eventually breaks.

Instead, I'm more accustomed to and comfortable with the

daily, often moment-to-moment crisis assessments of pallia-
tive care and hospice: the dread of inevitable death, the complicated machinery and endless paperwork of the hopelessly
sick and terminally ill, nurses and doctors traipsing in and
out of the house, trying to determine the "time line," which
is code for "how much time is left." A typical toddler tantrum feels illogical and foreign, but also unremarkable. I
don't belong in either community of mothers, not completely.
I am no longer just a bereaved parent, but a bereaved parent
with a living child. At Tay-Sachs family conferences, there is
usually a moment when we are asked to identify ourselves:
Who is bereaved? Whose child is living? I stand at the threshold between these two identities, and am beginning to understand that I always will. But will it always feel this
awkward? Sometimes I'm uncomfortable, sometimes confused, sometimes proud, and sometimes totally numb because I can't hold all of the emotions at once. Guilt is like a
blanket I drag around and sleep under and never wash. There
is no predicting when one of these emotions will arise and
how long it will last.

When Kent arrives home from work a few minutes later,
after a ten-hour workday as editor of a regional magazine
and a forty-minute commute in each direction, Charlie is
heaped in my lap, hair damp with sweat, face tear-streaked
and red. "Balloon," she whispers plaintively every few seconds and then snuggles into my armpit.

"What happened?" Kent asks, looking around. I sense his
irritation, and I feel it, too. In the hour I try to reserve daily
to contain the damage an active toddler can make, I've been
reading favorite books, offering Popsicles, producing magic

wands—all the crowd favorites. As a result, unwashed dishes sit in the sink gathering stink and crust; the kitchen floor is littered with dried-up spaghetti that feels like being poked with knives if you happen to step on it; books and checkers and Lego and pieces of cheap plastic toys are scattered everywhere; a few plastic cars precariously block entrances to rooms, one with a stuck horn playing the theme song from *Frozen* with a fading battery that renders it a funereal dirge. I feel inept and undone. I feel *ashamed*.

"Balloon," I say without thinking, and the wailing starts up again in earnest, with this new and highly sympathetic audience of one: Daddy. He runs over and scoops her up. The teachers at school gather in the doorway to watch Kent drop Charlie off in the morning. He hugs her, asks for another hug, another kiss, then she asks for another hug, another kiss, "Have me!" she cries, and then he waits and watches as she gallops into her friend group, his eyes brimming with tears. "Sometimes dads are anxious to get away," her teacher told me. "They just drop and go. But we love to watch how much he loves his girl."

With Charlie on his hip, Kent pours two big fingers of whiskey into a fat crystal glass at the sideboard. "Poor girlie," he says. She sniffles. And then, about the car, he asks, "Can you turn that thing off?"

"First," I reply, suddenly fuming, "I need to be able to get off the couch." I am a hot ball of irritation.

Charlie jumps from Kent's arms, and quickly forgetting the tragic events of the previous hour, opens the front door and solemnly reports that "someone is in trouble," her favorite game to play. "It's an emergency!" she cries gleefully, stumbling slightly over those last two syllables. In this game, one stuffed animal is tied up in a string or a cloth belt from one of my dresses and then dangled over the side of the porch to save the toy in trouble (alien toy, a member of the Paw Patrol, an occasional Barbie, although this last toy I'd prefer to leave in the dirt).

I sit perfectly still, feeling the sweat cool against my skin, my thighs stuck to the leather couch cushions.

"You okay?" Kent asks. "Why don't you relax while I go help save some animals?" (Or, as Charlie says, "the aminals.")

I nod. He and Charlie make their way to the porch. The grandfather clock marks out the time evenly behind me. I listen to Charlie instruct her father about exactly how to lower the pink doggy on the rope to save the stuffed owl, who has *broken his eye*. "Not his wing?" I hear Kent ask. No, it's his eye. Her sweet, almost cartoonish voice; his deep voice. The mix of their laughter.

I know what I have: this beautiful girl whom, four years ago, I never could have imagined. I didn't look at the developmental milestones chart when Ronan was alive because I knew he'd never meet them; with Charlie, who is smart, beautiful, healthy, funny, kind, and curious, I don't look at the charts because I know I don't have to worry about it. She loves books, has full conversations (and heated arguments) with us, and is, as her teacher reported during her school conference, "a really good friend." She's the child I always wanted (of course, so is everybody's child), but it doesn't mean I wanted Ronan less, even after his diagnosis, or that I miss him less, even though Charlie would not exist if Ronan had been healthy, if he had lived, or if he'd had the single enzyme programmed into his tangle of DNA that would have saved his life. Two halves of one life, the C-section incision out of which both children were lifted, two bodies from a body cut at its center. The two mothers.

Ronan was, in fact, the one who led me to Kent, the father of this girl who wouldn't exist if her brother were not lost to me. A journalist, Kent had read a piece I'd written about Ronan while he was still living, but already blind and entering a period of drastic decline, and his father and I had been split for some time. Kent asked me to lunch. I hadn't realized we were Facebook friends. "Look at all that hair!" my friend Lisa said when I told her Kent and I had a kind-of date. "And he's right in your age bracket!"

We met at a Santa Fe café famous for blue cornmeal pancakes and strong, sweet coffee. Kent was wearing his sunglasses on a string around his neck, and he did have fantastic salt-and-pepper hair, tons of it. He was tall and solid and wore cowboy boots with his initials (KB) stitched on the back of each. The first thing he said to me was "I just had a dream where all of my teeth fell out. What do you think it means?" I laughed, really laughed, for the first time in two years, a feeling so unfamiliar it made me blush. "You're anxious?" I responded, feeling this new and strange lightness. "Oh, totally," he said. "Who isn't?"

A few weeks later, on our first "night" date ("That makes it definitely a date-date," Lisa mused), Kent asked me how my family had supported me, and I told him that my parents had been amazing, but others had withdrawn, finding it "too hard," or "not knowing what to say." Kent considered for a moment over his drink (which he insisted later was watered down), looked up at me with bright, clear blue eyes, and said, "That must feel like a betrayal. That's really hard." Exactly. We had dinner (he forgot his glasses so I had to read the menu and the bill aloud to him), and I learned that he was twenty years older than I (fifty-eight, not forty-eight, and far out of what I considered to be my acceptable dating age bracket) and was getting ready to leave Santa Fe (he owned a hundred-year-old church he had grown weary of endlessly renovating). He was an excellent listener, even when I was so nervous, talking so fast. When we walked back to his car parked in front of the Hotel Saint Francis, we noticed it had a dent in the side. A hit and run. "What do you think it means?" he asked. "Worlds collide!" I offered. He laughed.

I was smitten, for sure, but it was when I introduced Kent to Ronan that I understood I was falling in love against reason and all the odds. Kent walked right up to Ronan, who was immobile then, sitting propped up in his high chair, where he spent a great deal of time. Kent knelt down, touched Ronan's feet and then his hands, and said, "Oh, hey there, buddy. You're a big guy, aren't you?" and then he kissed his face. It was a father's voice, from a man who had always wanted to have children.

Just as trauma and grief unmake the world, love remakes it. This family life—Kent's, Charlotte's, and mine—so traditional, seemingly so effortless for others—was everything I thought I'd never have only three short years ago, so how can I possibly become so undone and unnerved by a temper tantrum, a lost balloon, or a ruined carton of eggs? Who cares? This is trivial business compared to my other parenting experience: seizure meds in small syringes, the liquid parceled out in millimeters; dread like a wall to climb over every morning; and hospice nurses and oxygen and suction machines and hours spent watching my child wither and fade from Tay-Sachs disease. I survived the *death of my child* and now I'm losing my shit over normal toddler behavior and feeling stressed out by a stack of dirty dishes? Sure, an annoying day, but not an *unbearable* one, which certainly described some of the toughest days with Ronan, including the day of his death, and yet I had borne them because there had been no other choice. Ronan taught me that life is about being present with each moment, that the future is a mystery, the past is unfixable, and that it's in the present where we truly *live* and thrive. Everything else is unreal, ephemeral, and more often than not, a lie. Ronan was my teacher, my guru, my first baby, my boy. I feel ungrateful, unaware, ridiculous, *guilty*. Have I so quickly unlearned all the lessons that being his mother taught me?

When Ronan was alive, I would have given anything for a day like this. My response to any parent who told a story similar to the one I've just described would have been anger and desperation (and, I must admit, delivered smugly, and meant to land like a wound): "You should be so lucky to be irritated by a tantrum. At least your kid isn't dying." This was a highly effective way to stop the conversation, which was precisely the point. I couldn't bear the mundane stories about people's normal struggles on the planet of parenthood from which I had been, I believed, permanently exiled.

The two lives I have lived in such close proximity to each other—in the span of two years losing a child and a marriage, then marrying again and having another child, one life braiding with the other, sometimes colliding, getting tangled together—hits me with a physical, full-body *wallop*.

Not so long ago I was trying to figure out how to work a suction machine in case I needed to drain Ronan's fluid-filled lungs. After his father moved out, Ronan slept next to me in my big bed, immobile save for seizures, silent save for moans that might indicate pain that nobody could decipher. *We just don't know a lot about the brain* was the response I received from all the brain specialists and doctors I researched on the Internet and to whom I sent desperate, middle-of-the-night emails asking for answers. I traced Ronan's spine, sometimes for hours at a time, working to memorize a sensation now lost to me. Now Charlie takes up most of the middle of the king bed, sleeping always in a dress *and* socks and shoes, and either on my back, snuggled under my armpit, or coiled around my head. A living child. The new normal, or perhaps the new confusing.

I love Charlie as fiercely in life as I love her brother in death. The boy and the girl share only one characteristic— long, blond eyelashes—which means that Charlie reminds me of Ronan only when she sleeps. Only then do I notice their resemblance to each other: the soft cheeks, the gentle countenance, the spidery eyelash shadows on the pillow. In these moments I feel as if I hold both children at once. The living girl and the missing boy: siblings only in imagination, alive together only in the grief house of memory, a structure impermeable as brick and insubstantial as a paper wall.

Is it truly a collision of lives, this one and the other? Or is it parallel lives experienced side by side, a fulfillment of that promise stitched on a church banner from my childhood? Or are these experiences lived one on top of the other, the lines flipping vertical, sometimes horizontal, and sometimes crossing each other? Could it be that one way of living, one way of being, the life with one child, is absorbed inside or alongside the life with another? I know that once you've carried a child inside of you, his or her DNA stays in your body forever, a few free-floating cells that remain until they die with you, and then, too, they live on in some way—as molecules, or as that mysterious, invisible *stuff* of the world scientists call dark matter that cannot be proven to exist and yet we move through as we move through air—every day and all the time.

Dark matter itself is invisible and undetectable, and yet astrophysicists believe it is potentially responsible for adding gravity to galaxies; the amount of visible material in galaxies simply cannot explain the quality and frequency of their shapes and movements. Collections of stars form galaxies, and galaxies organize into clusters. Using visible light telescopes, scientists can see the space between galaxies if it is filled with gas hot enough to appear as X-rays or gamma rays. The result: There is more material in the clusters than can be detected. This invisible matter was first called "dark matter" in the 1930s by Swiss astronomer Fritz Zwicky. The measured speed of revolution of a galaxy, which depends on the weight and position of matter in the cluster, suggested more mass than observable light revealed. This result was confirmed in the 1970s by U.S. astronomer Vera Rubin in her studies of galaxy rotation.

Scientists continue to debate the consistency and makeup of dark matter, although all agree that our very existence is dependent on this material for which there is no definitive, empirical proof. We live and move, necessarily, even unconsciously, according to a faith in the world. We absorb that faith as we live and breathe, without effort or even definitive knowledge. Dark matter: thought to make up nearly 85 percent of the matter in the universe, undetectable because it emits no light and cannot be directly observed, possibly made of subatomic particles scientists are still seeking to identify.

Still, dark matter is defined more by what it is not than by what it might be. Dark matter could be many things: "failed" stars, or remnants of the cores of dead small stars. It could be a black hole, or what's left after a large star explodes or comes apart. Scientists study dark matter indirectly by looking at shadows and trying to figure out what causes it. Dark matter: the great mystery of the universe that we move through every day without conscious thought. DNA: the mysterious puzzle we have yet to fully solve, that dictates who we are, how we live, and even, sometimes, when we die.

Charlie and Ronan will only ever coexist in this energy-dense air, and in their most primitive forms, as cells dividing inside the darkness of my body, or as threads of coded helix crossing in the chaos of my blood—the same blood that carried Tay-Sachs.

Kent and Charlie are singing a song on the porch about the turtle that jumps into the bathtub and the lady with the alligator purse. Charlie corrects Kent's lyrics several times. "No, Daddy. Listen to me. It's like this."

I want to get out there in the now, but I also want to remember, that great act of invention that keeps the dead alive, if only in our imagination. Or, as Joy Williams writes in *The Changeling*: "Memory is the resurrection. The dead move among us, the living, in our memory, and that is the resurrection."

Maybe it's these false divisions of time that are the issue; maybe this is what stops me when people insist that I have a "new life," which sounds like the Christian notion of the "afterlife"—that life wiped clean of what has come before, whether it be physical ailment or trouble or despair or sinfulness. This doesn't seem even remotely realistic, and no longer appeals to me, even from a faith-based perspective. Can happiness be pure without the promise of unhappiness perpetually alive inside it? Happiness: so fierce, and yet so delicate. *On a sheer peak of joy we meet/Below us hums the abyss;/ Death either way allures our feet/If we take one step amiss* (Edith Wharton, "A Meeting"). There is no new versus old life; instead, one exists in the shadow of the other, perhaps in its continuing light, like stars that are seen only after they've long exploded and died, and yet they sit in the sky still, marking our ordinary time, which is always an extraordinary mix of times. "Two things have to be happening at once in every narrative moment," I preach to my writing students. So why do we think life is any different? Why don't we have the tools to absorb the past rather than pretend that we can let it go or move beyond it? I miss my son's face and his small self. In my mind I carry him wherever I go, feeling his weight, his softness, his helplessness, his light. This isn't "baggage" to be set down, or "damage" to be repaired and forgotten. It's love, which we can carry in so many forms, and all at once, in every moment.

. . .

Yet I hadn't anticipated the forgetting, giving in to this idea that the one life would recede—with all its strange terrors and unexpected glories—and a new life would emerge, one that appears, from the outside, like a fairy tale of love. The headline: "Twice divorced thirty-eight-year-old mother with a dying child falls in love with a fifty-eight-year-old bachelor living in a renovated, possibly haunted church in a town of a few hundred hippies in rural New Mexico." It's like the log line for one of the romantic comedies I can't stand but agree to watch when my girlfriends insist upon it.

I didn't think I'd need to stitch together scenes and impressions from the past as the present is unfolding, didn't predict how unsettling and strange and also necessary this would feel. I didn't anticipate feeling so divided, so lost. Although I think about Ronan every day, it is sometimes difficult to remember the silence and stillness of his body when Charlie is so busy, so active, so able to do all of the things that were completely out of reach for her half brother in his short life. She walks easily along balance beams, sprints into the surf at the beach, dances to songs from *The Little Mermaid* and announces, "Hey. These are my moves. Watch me." One morning after dropping her off at preschool I stood and watched her through a crack in the gate. She ran up to an empty swing and flopped her belly on top, swinging back and forth and smiling. She did it again and again. "Charlie's so verbal," her teacher tells me. "So good with her body. So strong, so smart."

When I'm out with Charlie in the world, people ask me all the time, in the grocery store, in the queue at the post office, after commenting, always, on the red of her hair (*So beautiful! So rare!*): "Is she your only child? Will you have more?

Was it just one and done?" and I have to make a choice. Do I tell them about Ronan and launch into the pain of that past; or do I say nothing, which triggers a different kind of guilt and pain? When I don't say his name, I feel like I'm erasing him; when I do, I have to buckle up for a conversation that usually ends in someone patting me on the back and saying, "You're so brave." Each option makes me crumble a little inside. If I'm not keeping Ronan's memory alive by acknowledging him each time I'm given the opportunity, am I forgetting him, letting him go, which is like sentencing him to a kind of second death?

Memory, with its strange and extraordinary power to make and unmake the world, is perhaps itself an accident of evolution. What is forgotten inside what is remembered? How do we pluck the most significant moments out of the rank and file of ordinary memories? These two children, one so different from the other. Does this make me two different mothers? Two different women leading two wildly different lives? Must I separate them? Should I just forget that the other woman, with a different husband, a different child, living a totally different life, ever existed? I don't think so. Perhaps we can live our best lives only in the moments when past and present converge and recombine, like in the coiled DNA helix. Maybe we live well only when we understand that our lives are always spinning inside chaos, with possibilities both wondrous and catastrophic moving side by side within even the tiniest revolution. Maybe we have to live all of our lives, in all of their pain and joy, all at once and at the same time. What is required for us to do that?

CHAPTER TWO

Against Bravery

To all who say I can't imagine what
you must be feeling, *to those who ask that
question:* How'd you survive? *say* brave, *say* but
I'd never be able to manage what

you have, *I say no. Climb up with me now,
saddle up this grief, imagine. Here's how
we stay human even torched by sorrow:
stare at my (it might be your) tomorrow,*

*ride back to the whisper of his baby
laugh, two milk teeth, silky feet, life maybe
contained in what we call* gone, *but give me
this: feel of his belly, slippery,*

*swimming in my arms, give me each sweet note
of his breathing—imagine us—afloat.*

RACHEL DEWOSKIN, FROM "IMAGINING"

"Congratulations on the resurrection of your life," a col-
league wrote to me just after Charlie's birth in March
2014. I was taken aback, and before typing a quick response
to this arresting opening line, I stopped, considering. I'd
heard "second chance," and *it's like you have a whole new life,*

and *your life is beginning again*, but this word, "resurrection," evoked the image of beginning again in a much more immediate way.

I am not made new; I am not "over" the loss of my son, and in that sense I have risen like no phoenix, been resurrected like no god. These are myths, which by their nature are imaginary frameworks: nobody actually *lives out* these stories. Why, then, would anyone be expected to? Instead, I am two people, one person divided, alive within the same body, trying to reconcile one life with the other, adjusting to a new baseline, trying to keep a foot squarely at the threshold between past and present.

During the two years Ronan was dying, I unwittingly became the poster child for resilience, a word with which I've always had a complicated relationship. "I would die if I were you" I'd hear at the grocery store, or in the pharmacy line as I waited for Ronan's seizure medication to be mixed and bottled. "You are tragic, he is tragic, it's all so tragic." I'm sure I was polite, or maybe I wasn't, but inside I was railing, reeling. My secret desire was to punch these strangers in the face. A few times I came close to doing just that.

Tragedies are narratives with no place to go, no alternative endings to choose or create. No open doors, no thresholds, no light. They are narrative prisons, and I didn't need or want to be reminded of that when each day my son's life disappeared into a lightless, impenetrable, locked-down cell that I could not enter to provide comfort. He suffered; I could not relieve it. In the next breath, these same people (well-wishers?) would praise me, which felt as jarring and disorienting as being labeled tragic. "You're more resilient than you know." "This is a test of your resilience." "You can do it." "Be strong."

"Oh yes," I'd say. "Yes, of course. Thank you." And then I'd sit in my car and push my forehead against the steering wheel, enraged and confused, saying aloud to nobody, "I didn't ask for a fucking test." I blubbered and sputtered in the hot sun or in the blast of the car heater, snot falling into my lap, sweaty hands gripping the wheel as if I could tear it free. I was not thankful for the chance to remind someone else about how terrible life could be, or how lucky they were that they had avoided my singular, shitty fate. I didn't want to put other people's lives "in perspective." "I couldn't do it, but you're so resilient. You're so strong." I was not. I was a mess. I was so sad I couldn't believe I managed to be upright at all during the day. I was also still alive, but the thought of being brave and powerfully resilient *for the rest of my life,* or held up as an example of strength, left me exhausted and bewildered. That, I knew, was unsustainable, not to mention an inaccurate description of my state of mind and body.

I was so weary of the labels "brave" and "courageous." From Sonali Dev's *A Distant Heart:* "Keep courage. Courage. That's what they kept calling it. This thing they wanted him to keep. But how did you keep something you did not own? Did not know? Could not find in the hungry panic inside you?" My "hungry panic," not bravery or courage, drove me to write. I wasn't brave for telling my story; I was simply doing the only thing I knew how to do, the only work I've ever loved. And I wasn't doing it because I possessed some extraordinary courage, as if I were holding a glass ball inside my heart, protecting it, caring for it; I was doing it because it was necessary. This was a chop wood, carry water scenario. There were strong and irritating parallels with the "overcoming disability" trope I'd been resisting my entire life. I was applauded for being out in the world with a disability; I was *so brave* for living in the body I was given, as if I'd been given any other choice.

After Ronan died and I had another baby, I heard the words "brave" and "courageous" again, but I also just as often heard "resilient." A word like a woodpecker—insistent and impossible to ignore. People continued to congratulate me for being "so brave and so resilient," for being "so strong." I was happy, but I was still gutted from the loss of my son, from the way in which he died, from the manner in which my previous marriage ground to an unexpectedly acrimonious end. I wasn't strong, and I wasn't brave. I was not in a war, and I wasn't fighting any battles. Couldn't I just be a normal human being who had suffered a traumatic loss? Wasn't it enough to still be moving through the world and stringing words together? Wasn't that, in fact, the story *everyone* would live if they survived long enough to lose a beloved?

So the word "resilient" didn't fit. It was as if I'd put on a dress that didn't suit me, and when I walked out of the dressing room everyone told me how great I looked, and I knew these compliments were lies. The word was a badge that had been pinned to me, only I hadn't earned it, and had no interest in doing so. I just wanted to live my extraordinary life in an ordinary way, as we all do. What did it actually mean to be set apart or made special in this way by this particular word? Words, of course, carry great power. Emily Dickinson said, "I know nothing in the world that has as much power as a word. Sometimes I write one, and I look at it, until it begins to shine." Or, in my case, I had looked at and heard the word so often it had become a burden and was beginning to rot.

I started to hear about resilience everywhere, it seemed, and I realized that it has become so much a part of the vernacular as to have practically become interchangeable with "strength" or "toughness." It is used widely and indiscriminately to describe everything from cities, politicians, children, and marriages to social movements, fabric, diseases, and even cells and tissues of the body. It is understood (or perhaps misunderstood) as a synonym for "grit," or "perseverance," as a character trait that stems from a person's individual will, from a self-directed ability to "bounce back." The word is deployed as a diagnostic tool for all kinds of situations, set forth as an achievable goal or state of mind, touted as the solution to all sorts of problems, from communities struggling to recover after an earthquake, to "at-risk" kids fighting to succeed despite education in subpar, underfunded schools.

When I stepped back from the bridge in Taos, I made a decision to live, although I had no clue—no map—of how to begin that journey. "You're so resilient; you'll find a way." This wasn't helpful or encouraging. Brave. Resilient. Strong. These are just words, but of course words are never just words, and truly understanding a word is not just a matter of semantics.

If the words "strong" and "resilient" and "brave" were treated as nearly interchangeable, did that mean they were, in fact, synonymous? No. That didn't feel right. Even if the words had similar meanings, none of them fit what I was or felt. What I wish I'd said to those people who described me as resilient when Ronan was dying: *I can't do it, either.* I almost didn't. And then, after Ronan died, to be applauded again for this mysterious quality of "resilience," the sign of which was an equally mysterious state of "moving on," which could be detected in what way? Through my perceived happiness? Also incorrect. I could spend a lifetime trying to "come to terms" with what happened, and I would always fail; to succeed would be to kill off that other mother who had chosen to live, to strap myself to those train tracks on a hot midwestern night and let the train flatten me into the ground. To "get over it," a feat so often expected of those who grieve, was an impossible goal. If I tried to do it I would be unable to do anything at all. I didn't want to nix "resilience" from my vocabulary, but I wanted to create space around this word, turn it over, turn it around. "The opposite of language is not silence/but space" (Jenny George, "The Gesture of Turning a Mask Around").

Now, in my current life, on the other side of what was a great fire that shaped and forged me in remarkable ways, I realize what I need to do. I need to dig to the bottom of the word "resilience," pull it up by its historical and etymological roots and have a look, because if it wasn't and isn't helpful to me—if its misuse was and is harmful in some real and fundamental way—then the same might be true for others. Children die every day; people lose their partners every day; mothers and fathers are buried every day. We need this word—it has texture and meat and nuance and shadow and light and blood in it—but we need a better understanding of what it means before we can use it for anyone's benefit, including our own.

I join Kent and Charlie on the porch, where Charlie is still saving "aminals," so I kneel behind her, give her a hug, and tell her I love her. "Okay, Mommy," she says, and turns to face me. "You're my best friend." I tap her little freckled nose with my finger and say, "Boop!" which she loves. "You bet I am. Always." I feel it in me, that uncomplicated, devastating happiness; it is as true and tactile as anything I've ever felt. But behind that feeling lurks the panic that the world can drop out from beneath your feet at any time, because that's true, too. Lightning can strike the same place twice, three times; it can strike you all your life. Knowing this, how do we keep living?

CHAPTER THREE

The Long Winter

This is how a child dies:
little by little. His breath
curdles. His hands
soften, apricots
heavy on their branches.

I can't explain it.
I can't explain it.

On the walk back to the car
even the stones in the yards
are burning. Far overhead
in the dead orchards of space
a star explodes
and then collapses
into a black door.

This is the afterlife, but
I'm not dead. I'm just
here in this field.

JENNY GEORGE, "DEATH OF A CHILD"

It is not possible to accurately record a child's death; the record will always be inaccurate, half of a half of the whole story, but it is this origin story that underlies all the stories that follow: every laugh, every triumph, every moment of peace.

First, a death.

The time of my son's death was 2:32 A.M. on February 15, 2013. He died of GM2 gangliosidosis: "a rare inherited disorder that progressively destroys nerve cells (neurons) in the brain and spinal cord." Tay-Sachs disease. I sometimes imagined the slick-limbed skeletons in the chilly corners of the orthopedic clinic waiting rooms of my childhood. I saw them lit and burning, the flames moving quickly up the spine, reaching the brain last and spreading out like a fiery web, burning bone as if it were no more than grassland. A complete conflagration.

Ronan's death certificate records his time of death as 7:30 A.M.; at 2:40 A.M., when I called the hospice nurse, Cynthia, and begged, "Please don't call anyone yet," I was asking her to lie on the official record. She did.

Although Ronan had been declining and slowly diminishing quite dramatically during January, it was during the week of Valentine's Day, just when the weather became consistently bitter and incessantly gray, that he began the final stage of dying, or what's known as "actively dying," as if the damage his disease had done to this point was passive.

What I observed were the changes—some subtle, others more dramatic. His skin started to turn a mottled blue for five- and ten-minute labors of time, small agonies of time, before returning to its original pale color. These collections of minutes were little terror ships set to sail and then called back to shore, again and again. Our panic and calm traveled in waves. He had turned blue before, but only once, and that time we had held him upside down until the blood returned to his face. Now he was too delicate for that. We were simply waiting, which was the only kind of holding we could do. Sometimes a shadow crossed his face, a change in light so pronounced it produced the urge to turn around and see who (or what) was there.

Dark impressions began appearing under his eyes and then disappearing, as if they'd been pressed there and then suddenly erased, as if someone marked him, changed their mind, marked him again. A tube delivered fluids through his nose, what the hospice nurse referred to as a "comfort care" intervention. The little tube taped to Ronan's face trembled with each of his shallow breaths.

Those of us who loved Ronan dangled from each strange and precious moment. We made lunch, scraped the food into the trash, washed the dishes, put them away. We dumped laundry detergent over dirty clothes. We drank water and red wine and said "I love you" because it was the designated day to express such sentiments. When I couldn't stand the waiting, I would run and run and run to Eminem's rage-filled beats as if I were in training for a race. My jaw ached from being braced, as if I could fight grief with my face.

At night, I woke from sleep so shallow it was like a water bug gliding across a pond. I panicked, unable to open my mouth. I unlocked my jaw by rubbing it and breathing in and out slowly, and then I sat up.

"What if I need to scream?" I asked Kent—finally, in this impossible time, I had found a right match after so many of the wrong ones. "I can't swallow." I wanted to cry but couldn't. My neck ached, the roof of my mouth felt as if it were made of cracking plaster. Beads of sweat popped under my armpits and rose across my forehead.

Kent looked bewildered but pulled me to him. The grief therapist we'd been seeing since our second date had called him "a big strong man." I needed someone strong. I needed the solidity of him. I wanted him, this particular man, and had since the moment we'd met.

I had known him for such a short time. I had known him forever.

Ronan's father had moved out only a few months after our son's diagnosis, and the moment he left I was less lonely than I'd been for the past year. Now when he arrived at the house for his "care shifts," as we called them, blocks of time carefully arranged through a series of terse, information-only emails and the sharing of electronic, color-coded calendar months, I got in my car and drove as fast as I could to Kent's house, weeping with relief, heavy with guilt, but also lit from the inside with desire and anticipation and a feeling of being my best and truest self when I was with him—a self I thought had died. I would be half-undressed before I walked through the front door. "During the heavy months my life caught fire only when/I made love with you" (Tomas Tranströmer, "Fire Script"). You don't have to stoke the fire of grief. It is an easy conflagration. Flick an ember in the right direction at the right moment and watch it ignite. The same is true of love and lust, born, I believe, from grief's same blaze.

"Try not to worry," Kent said. Worry was indeed pointless at this stage. It was simply dread, the heart's cold sweat. The shades in the bedroom were drawn, but I had, on many nights alone in this bed, stared out at the bright swoop of the moon in the corner of the window as if it had been intentionally hung there, a magnet stuck to the sky. Sometimes it felt hopeful, other times as haunting as the line from Sylvia Plath's "Elm": "I know the bottom, she says. I know it with my great tap root: /It is what you fear." The snow on the ground, fossilized night after midwinter night, would melt slowly when the sun rose. The drains in the street, on the roof, would run with clear, cold water. So I longed for light, for movement and sound signaling morning, breath, and sunshine, but this also meant we were one step closer to the final change, that we'd grasped a new rung on the ladder and had now entered another stage of dying, so I dreaded it as well. Time was the keeper. Time was the enemy, the creator, the muse. Time was nothing at all, a useless and arbitrary metric.

According to Cynthia, with her cheery, booming voice, a woman I thought of as a walking, talking floral bouquet in her long, brightly colored skirts, it was, indeed, "only a matter of time" for Ronan. So we waited. "I'm praying to Jesus," she promised. *Jesus can't do shit for Ronan now*, I thought. *Just get the morphine ready.* She did. The clear liquid waited in syringes like arrows in a quiver, but there were other kids dying, too, and she sometimes had to answer her constantly ringing phone: "Call you right back," she'd shout into her phone and "Okay, I'll fax that prescription as soon as I can." It seemed as if she were speaking through a megaphone, like a middle-aged death cheerleader. I shifted between the de-sire to push her out the door and the desire to hold her, forever, in this room, by my side. If she stayed, Ronan stayed alive. Right? We could pause forever in this liminal state.

Of course we could not stay. The oxygen machine that had once bucked and hummed like a failing car engine sat silent in the closet, shoved in the corner next to the sleek green oxygen containers and the nebulizer, with its tiny pink tubes of saline secured inside a plastic bag. On the day of the first walk outside after Ronan died, my parents pulled down their coats from the closet, the zippers and buttons clanking against the hard apparatus of the sick, which now looked ridiculous and cruel, divested of its power and sandwiched between infinitely more useful winter boots and house slippers. It was like discovering a piece of a Viking ship in the closet. Like finding an electric chair in the city dump.

I asked Kent to *please take the machines away,* and he did. Everyone did everything I asked during those final days, but nobody could give me what I wanted, what I needed, what I had to have but could not have and would never have again: my son returned to me, his brain repaired, time unwound. I wanted nothing less than a new world and my son allowed to live within it.

The NO SMOKING ALLOWED sign pasted to the front window of the house and the laminated DO NOT RESUSCITATE order taped to the refrigerator in the kitchen were removed. The suction machine with its dangling tube was boxed and ready to be returned to the medical supply company.

We waited. All of the death paperwork had been filled out and lay stacked in a folder, although I didn't remember the answers to the questions: who would declare death, where the body would go, how long next of kin would stay with the body, et cetera. I heard my mom on the phone in the back room, where the gas fireplace produced a steady cone of heat, her voice quiet and tired, talking to a friend, telling her "Yes, yes, I know. We're here for the duration." The word felt thunderous and inevitable, the final curse for an already doomed boy.

It was midwinter in Northern New Mexico. A few cracked and frozen leaves fell to the ground and made a scraping sound or lay trembling, trapped by a typical wind made suddenly strange, in the brown yard or on the concrete sidewalk. The sky was a cruel cinder block above the adobe house where Ronan lay dying. C. S. Lewis said it best: "But oh God, tenderly, tenderly. Already, month by month and week by week you broke her body on the wheel whilst she still wore it. Is it not yet enough?"

According to Ronan's death certificate, a piece of light blue paper with a vaguely royal-looking imprint from the funeral home that must be presented to demonstrate, as the insurance company calls it, "proof of loss," my son was

Never married

Born on March 24, 2010

In possession of a social security number: 611-81-4007

Inactive in the armed forces, a member of no tribe. (Those boxes remained unchecked.)

He was a baby, then briefly a boy, and then, after the moment of his death, he was a decedent. Another way of saying it: gone.

He died, truly, of starvation or "wasting," his body no longer able to process food or liquids as it began to gradually shut down. We kept saying it, parroting the hospice nurse, as if using the right words mattered, a final stab at having any kind of authority about a process that nobody understood: "He looks like he's shutting down." We were all about to be shut out, some mysterious door made of iron, or of the heaviest wood—mahogany, cherry, oak, rough pine—closed between our world and wherever he was going.

On the last day of his life, Ronan weighed only eleven pounds. We had to be careful when we moved him so as not to dislocate his shoulders and hips, he was that bony, that delicate. His breath smelled sour and of the ground, and his mouth was locked open and unmoving. This was part of "the end stage," as the hospice nurses call it, those days and moments and hours when the body begins its process of unbinding; a life, however brief or long, loosening as all our lives will someday. Ronan was retreating, and there was nothing anyone could do to keep him behind. From dust to dust, but to where?

I wanted to take him outside a last time into the world he was about to leave forever. Shouldn't he feel the sun once more? Shouldn't the world with all its beauty see what it was about to lose from its dome of sounds and sights and smells? In my dreaming, delusional mother's mind I thought the world might provide some healing tonic, and any miracle that might happen would happen there, under the sky and with the trees as witnesses.

"He's been indoors for too long," I said, as if this were the overwhelming problem. "He needs fresh air." The hospice nurse told me gently that he was too weak to go. Only a week before this Kent had carried Ronan to the coffee shop in the front pack, limbs hanging loose, his little face turned up to the sun. A dark knot of birds rose into the sky and then broke apart like a firework, like a star, like disaster. The birds would go on, but Ronan would never see the sun again. I was glad now that I'd taken a picture.

"You want him to die at home," Cynthia carefully reminded me, as I had stated this wish repeatedly and sometimes forcefully over the last two years while we constructed and revised Ronan's "plan of care," the most miserable document I've ever written or revised. I understood that Ronan's end was so near he might die outside, in the cold. "Okay," I said, but I insisted on opening a window, then said nothing when, after a few moments, the nurse gently eased it shut. The next time Ronan left this house, he would be dead.

When I sat with Ronan, I had the impulse to put my hands out in the air, take some kind of heroic action. Now I would take on the mantle of "brave." Now I would do anything. What would I do? Pull him back? Push him forward? He clearly wanted to go; his eyes were fixed on some unseen target. I had difficulty, in those final days, determining the difference between faith and imagination. "He's not going to heaven! There is no God!" I'd shout at my father, a Lutheran pastor, although he never once mentioned where Ronan might be going. "All right, all right," he'd say, moving his hands together and apart as if opening and closing a curtain.

Although nothing could be made better, people tried to make it better, often unsuccessfully. When Cynthia said, "It's only eighteen inches between the head and the heart, but that's a long distance when it comes to death," I wanted to bite her, suck out her good feeling, drain the color from her clothes. Later, she would be the only one who could comfort me, she who had lost a child in an accident, her young son falling to his death from a roof while on a church trip in Mexico, a woman who left her family to sleep two nights in a cheap hotel in Santa Fe to be near us when we needed her, responding within seconds to a text or a phone call, no matter what time it was.

The "duration" lasted longer than we anticipated. Although Cynthia encouraged us to stop fluids and let our son die, Ronan's father didn't want to comply; unwilling, at the end, to admit that he was not prepared, although how could anyone be? We were at an impasse, our final one as parents, as people. I was afraid to cause conflict in these last hours of Ronan's life, a decision I will always regret. "You disgust me," Ronan's father had told me. "You're hysterical and crazy." When he said this to me, although I felt the same way about him and about myself, I didn't say a word. Instead I stood up and went into what was once our bedroom and shut and locked the door. I sat on the bed and shook with rage, with shock, with hate, which made me feel wild and weak, like sprinting on an empty stomach, fearing my legs would buckle beneath me, the body inadequately fueled. The world had made kindness impossible, it seemed, and I wanted to turn away from all of it. In Ronan's final days I couldn't bear to hear—or to say—any more cruel words, so I said nothing and Ronan suffered. For this I do not forgive myself, or Ronan's father.

Every small bone in Ronan's face became visible. He became as hollow as a reed, this fading instrument of my boy. I could circle his arms and thighs by touching my thumb and pinkie finger together, and this physical act, so simple for me, requiring no thought, was a movement so advanced for Ronan's devastated brain that he was never able to do it.

Finally, his father came around and agreed to stop all fluids but morphine. "I prayed to Jesus for a miracle and he granted it," Cynthia said tearfully, and she was so adamant, so good, that I almost believed her and was almost near tears myself, even though my heart was calm in my chest, a cold, dumb rock. Ronan lived for three days after fluids were stopped. He always had a strong heart, a powerful heartbeat from his first sonogram, but in those final hours it did him no favors.

I fell asleep at some point during the vigil, and while my mom was rocking him in the other room, Ronan breathed out for the final time through the last of the morphine drip. When she called my name, "Emily!" I knew what had happened. I ran to them.

In the middle of the cold night, the windows dark, the house completely still and yet also, it felt to me, poised to crash around us, I stood in the mouth of the world— motionless but far from restful. I was falling, and yet everything felt too calm, too still. The sun had not yet risen. When it did rise my son, my only child, my firstborn, would be dead. He had, as Teju Cole describes it, gone through the process of being permanently unselved. It was over. All the moments the two of us had shared added up to this final forever moment that would stay like a hook in my life, pulling up old wounds and tearing new ones, an insistent, prickling drag. *This is woe,* I thought. The house of my life had collapsed. "When suddenly a mighty wind swept in from the desert and struck the four corners of the house. It collapsed on them and they are dead, and I am the only one who has escaped to tell you!" (Job 1:19). Except that the house had not collapsed; we were not dead. The four of us remained upright, hunched over Ronan's still form.

My parents were huddled together, stooped and weeping. "Oh, sweet boy," my mom said. There were Kent's hands on my shoulders. I didn't touch Ronan, but instead knelt before him, swallowing again and again. I stood up and moved over to the couch, as if that would undo what had happened. Where was Jesus with his Lazarus touch? I, the nonbeliever, wishing, praying I could make it happen. I was trembling, but my eyes were dry when I blinked. Had I expected some last-minute divine intervention? I felt unexpectedly stupid, and shamed, and knew this was not the right reaction.

"Take him," my mom gently implored, but I could not. I shook my head. If I took him, he would be dead, and after two years of preparing for this moment, I was now wretched with disbelief. "No," I said. "I can't take him. I won't take him." I stared at the coffee table, where Cynthia's daily cups of half-finished coffee had left interlocking circles across the wood, visible markers of minutes and hours, rings on a tree. Each time she left, her perfume lingered in the air and made Ronan sneeze. "He sneezed," I said now. "I heard him."

"No," my mom said softly. "No, Emily. He's gone."

Kent took Ronan into his lap and immediately began to sob. "Take the tube out!" he shouted, and my mom slid the skinny tube from Ronan's nose and that's when I grabbed Ronan and held him. He was still. His body was weighted with absence. His breath was gone. Belief set in then, together with a darkness that felt bigger and more textured and complicated than the one filling in the windows. And then I cried, although it came out like a high wail, a wave of solid sound I had never made before, a sound that was a part of the world, evoking a long history of women losing their children from this hateful disease and many others. "It is like the keening sound the moon makes sometimes,/rising" (Robert Hass).

After death, that silence: a whitewash of stillness as if a feeling could be painted on the walls. "Now I understand why people believe the soul departs with the last breath," Gloria Steinem writes in *My Life on the Road.* "Everything is the same, yet everything is different."

We sat for what seemed like minutes, but was in fact hours; hours to wash and dress and touch the body, and I know I did this but I remember none of it. The hospice nurse called the funeral home, and the "representatives" arrived in a gray minivan, the kind that soccer moms drive to games, to the store, to school pickup. Normal moms without dead kids. Normal moms with living kids who thought they had problems. We called Ronan's father and he arrived at the house.

The sky brightened to a fierce and stupid winter blue after a series of gray days. Moments before the van arrived, I went in to sit with Ronan and I touched Ronan's father on the arm, as we looked down at our dead boy. I wanted to make peace, maybe even a connection, here at this final hour, but he shook me off and pulled the hood of his sweatshirt around his face. He turned his back to me, kept one hand on Ronan's foot, our child disappearing, it seemed, inside his white shroud, cold and growing colder.

"I will carry him," the undertaker promised in the heavy quiet of Ronan's nursery—pink walls, posters of happy clowns, a changing table, a closet full of clothes—where his shrouded body lay in the crib. I had picked out that piece of Irish linen with my friend Tara a year before and asked her to embroider Ronan's name on it in blue and green. *This one,* I said in the store, handing her the bolt to cut, *this one.* Fierce Arizona sunlight struck the windows of the fabric store and Tara set her hand on my back. The night before this one I had pulled the fabric from the bag where it had been stored and carefully laid it out, remembering how Tara held the bolt straight and the clean sound of the scissors through the linen as I cut.

"I will keep him in the front with me," the undertaker said. "I will keep watch." She had long, veined fingers and wore her dark hair in braids, like a young girl. We lifted him up. His body was light, so light, yet heavy as the newly dead.

I stood with Ronan's father in the doorway of the house where we had lived unhappily together, and we watched the mortuary van drive away, our final act as parents to our child. A boy lost forever and for good. I wiped my dry mouth over and over again until my lips began to burn. I had a strange memory of a woman who held my forehead in a New York City subway station in 1992 while I puked up a pitcher of beer over a line of rats marching across the train tracks, and then handed me a fistful of tissues to wipe my mouth. Who was she? She was wearing an orange sweater. She had clean hands. Why that memory in this moment? My heart was a rubber band connected to the spoke of the van's wheel—straining, stretching, then snapping.

The van finally turned the corner slowly with Ronan inside and disappeared. Ronan's father left the house. It was the last time I would see either one of them.

The air was biting cold, but as the sun strengthened, a few brave birds hopped from branch to branch in the frozen trees, beating their wings so quickly it was as if they, too, were shivering. Ronan was diagnosed in a winter of record cold; it was another cold winter when he died. My father stood in the yard, alone, looking out. My mom sat hunched over herself on the couch, as if being smaller would make the pain less intense, and said, "I hate it when they take them away," as if evoking the whole world of the dead, of which Ronan was the newest member.

My friend Julia, who had swooped me up into a new circle of friends after my marriage ended, came to the house weeping, holding two bags of bagels. She stood in the doorway and kissed my face. Another friend brought sparkling water and laughter. We slept. Months ago I had told Kent that I never wanted to spend another night in that house after Ronan died, and I never did. Tara arrived later that day and helped me give away half of my closet. "That looks like something you'd wear to the Renaissance fair," she admitted. "Too much animal print," she said, tossing a cheetah-print tank top into the pile of items headed to Goodwill. She made me laugh, which felt both terrible and new, a reminder of what people did when they were not gripped by grief.

"I'll take care of everything," Kent had promised me, and he did. We left the house that night, he and I, and slept in his bed, which had become our bed; in the turn-of-the-century church where he had lived and which had become our home. Over the next week he moved all of my furniture and belongings to the church. He took the garbage bags full of clothes to Goodwill, and stacked couches and chairs and plates and mugs my parents had packed into the back of his truck and drove them down Highway 30—past the prison, then the charter school, then the hospice sanctuary for old and rejected animals where I'd once taken Ronan to pet the sad, abandoned dogs and aging horses, through the rocky high desert that gave way to hills spotted with sagebrush, and then through Cerrillos with its adobe church tower and on to Madrid with its colorful street signs and dogs roaming free.

Here was a beginning. I felt this in the small, hopeful place that had been ignited on my very first date with Kent, only six months before, in August, and only weeks after I stepped back from the River Gorge Bridge in Taos, just weeks after I had decided not to jump. We would make a life together, as frightened as I was that I was already too damaged, too ruined, to live at all. Now, here I was. Here we were. And we were good and we were in love.

But I had lost my child, my boy. I was nobody's mother. And what good is a mother whose baby has suffered and died?

This, then, was the wreckage from which we were expected to rise. I received cards that were full of condolences, of course, and many that also asked me to be brave, to be strong, to move forward, to "remember my resilience." I ripped them up and threw them away. Words were useless. "What else is language/now but injury" (Allison Benis

White, "Waldgeist"). And it was only injury I saw; only damage I imagined. I wanted a card that would scream when you opened it and then immediately shatter.

After Ronan died, the nursery was dismantled, but that is too gentle a word. Instead, I saw it crumble: the clatter of nails falling to the floor as the clown poster I never liked was wrenched from the wall. The shimmy of loose glass in frames. The crack of the crib's wood, made of dark mahogany and carefully assembled only three years before, covered by a sheet printed with dancing monkeys and zebras and bears. I saw all the clothes save the outfit Ronan died in thrown into a box, heard the snarl and stick of the tape wrapping them up.

From this carnage of items, each object the beginning of a memory I couldn't follow without unraveling, I kept a single red mitten, a bag full of reddish brown hair from Ronan's first and only haircut, and the shirt that I cut from his body after his death, a toddler's pajama top with rockets and planets arranged in a whimsical pattern, a little boy's dream of space. I spent long, miserable afternoons digging through boxes and file cabinets and random drawers, looking for the matching space pants. Surely, surely I would have saved them. Where were the space pants? I never found them.

One Sunday morning in March I filed the record of Ronan's death in the same file with his birth certificate; two pieces of paper dated less than three years apart, a span so short it generated a dizzying surge of rage. The great brevity of my son's life, what Teju Cole has described as "a space of unfinished histories." Oh, I was angry. If a person, a ghost, an apparition had walked through the door and told me it was the personification of Tay-Sachs, I would have strangled it, gleefully, easily, with my bare and trembling hands. I had no place to set down my rage, so for a time I set it down on myself.

Ronan had no descendants. He did have survivors. But for the longest, ever-lengthening length of time, I did not want to be one of them. Or, more accurately, I did not yet know how.

CHAPTER FOUR

Afterworld

Once there was a shock
that left behind a long, shimmering comet tail.
TOMAS TRANSTRÖMER, FROM "AFTER A DEATH"
TRANSLATED BY ROBERT BLY

The post office in Cerrillos, New Mexico, is a one-room building next to the Urgent Health Care Clinic that nobody in the area appears to trust. The parking lot is always deserted, apart from a blue sedan that may belong to the very bored or perhaps incompetent physician. The post office, however, is constantly busy; residents of the villages of Cerrillos and Madrid make daily stops to collect bills and ad circulars and packages, rocking up in beat-up trucks, run-down Corollas, shiny, restored vintage cars, growling motorcycles, and everything in between, tires spraying dirt and gravel as they hop from unpaved road to the blacktop leading out to Highway 30 that tracks across this part of New Mexico. The floor of this "postal shack," as Kent and I call it, is caked with red mud in the summer and slick with melted snow in the winter. All the mail is dusted with a thin veil of dirt, regardless of the season. I've had a mailbox here since Christmas. Lorene, the postmistress, reminds me that this officially marks my couplehood with Kent.

"That's right," I say, and uncharacteristically blush. I have been living with Kent in St. Anne's Church in Madrid since the day Ronan died. When I returned from book tour—where I read passages written while Ronan was still alive, passages about what it means to parent a child with no future—all of my clothes were folded and put away in even stacks, my books unpacked, and my jewelry untangled and carefully organized. Kent had discovered pairs of earrings that had been living in necklace knots for several years. My mismatched socks were laid out in neat rows. He'd even figured out how to fold my running tops with their built-in bras and complicated straps. "It took me twenty minutes and a lot of cursing," he admits.

Each day from my post office box I pull out armloads of carefully sealed cream envelopes from the National Tay-Sachs and Allied Diseases Associations (NTSAD)—notes that accompanied donations made in honor of Ronan. "To honor the life of a beautiful boy." "Thinking of you and loving you." "You were a wonderful mother." This last one hits me, as I am a mother no longer. I've just spent two months talking about the experience of mothering in a book I wrote about parenting, and now what? When my mother offers, "You'll always be his mother," I snap back that it's easy for her to express this because her kids are still alive. At this stage in my grieving, if your child isn't dying or hasn't recently died I believe you have nothing of value to say to me, nor I to you. I don't admit this to anyone but myself because it feels painful and bitter and true.

There are so many letters from the NTSAD that Lorene saves the overflow in carefully bound stacks wrapped in long rubber bands that break in half when I roll them off. I read all the letters and store them, tucked inside their envelopes, in a drawer; later, when we move to California, I move the sealed box from temporary house-sit to rental house to storage unit to new house. In that box is proof that Ronan is remembered, that he lived and was known by others, and I like the idea of keeping the box close, traveling with it as the caretaker of these good wishes and remembrances, but I don't want to open it. I keep it tightly sealed and well marked in black ink: TRIBUTES FOR RONES. On the box I drew a trumpet, which is the musical instrument I associate most with tributes. It was a sloppy trumpet, as I am no artist, but each time I picked up the box I heard in my head a regal-sounding trill, or a long, high note in the air. A single, sustained song in praise of my boy's brief—and by all accounts miserable—life.

I receive other mail from people I hardly know but who know my parents, or Kent, or found me in some other way—it seems you can find anyone's address if you work hard enough, even if it's in a little shoebox on a country road near a town of three hundred people. These letters from strangers (or half strangers, as some of the names I half recognize) I don't keep, as they seem to express a desire for me to provide details about my feelings, often coupled with vague offers of new or renewed friendship. I don't want new friends. I feel

private, and maybe for the first time in my entire life, enti-
tled to demand my privacy by choosing not to reply to an
email from someone I've never met who asks, "I wonder
what it's like for you now," in the weeks after Ronan's death,
a woman who is the parent of living children. "None of your
business" would be the polite version of a reply I never send.
People I know in name only want to come and visit, stay in
our house, *connect.* I don't want them there. I fear they will
expect to see a particular kind of grieving mother and find
the wrong one.

What is the correct look of grief? Expectations are bur-
densome for a griever. What about a mother who has lost her
child? If people claim they can't even think about such a
thing, then the expectations are that much more far-reaching,
impossible to decipher, and doubly maddening. I fear a
mother will talk about her children and I will throw a drink
in her face and refuse to apologize. I'm afraid I will be called
"resilient" and "strong" and "inspirational" and "brave"
and literally be sick. And there would be pity, of course,
which is helpful to nobody. Contact with others feels unsafe;
I am a kinetic combination of feeling too split open and
overly guarded. Just as I often feel like I'm in a freak show
when people look at my artificial leg and ask about it, this
feels like an emotional freak show. *Look at the one-legged
woman. Look at the sick child. Look at the grieving mother.*
My first wooden legs had visible hinges on the sides; the knee
mechanisms were, in prosthetic parlance, "exoskeletal." Yes,
this is grief: worn on the outside, leaving no place to hide;
everyone can see exactly how you move, how you feel, who
you are. No privacy here, no shelter or safety.

I feel immense gratitude for the adobe walls Kent built around the church years before he met me. I like the image of him packing the mud up the hill on his back and using his hands to form the shapes of the walls—tall, rounded, rough to the touch in parts and smooth in others. Add a moat and a watchful dragon, knights with weapons, some archers at the ready along the wall, disconnect the phone, and we're getting somewhere. I want a henge, a Neolithic circle with a bank and a ditch and high stones and wooden pillars. If henges are ritual sites for astronomical events (literally and metaphorically), what could signal a bigger shift than grief? My henge is St. Anne's Parish in Madrid, New Mexico. *Keep me safe,* I think, to nobody in particular, to the world, I suppose, although I know this is a pointless wish. Nobody's passage through the world can ever be safe, and I realize with clarity that this assurance of safety is a lie parents cling to about parenting. It's a lie people cling to about their own lives and the lives of others. Few people, it seems, fully understand that they will eventually die, as will their children, and everyone else they've ever known or loved.

I worry that some of these letter writers and instant friends might be unconscious or even deliberate grief stalkers, those people who want to be part of a deeply sad experience as a way of testing their own emotional limits without going under. This emotional voyeurism feels vampiric and disingenuous, and more than just irritating. It makes me sick to my stomach and fills me with a wild rage. So many of us don't get the option of dipping a toe in the water of extreme experience—instead we are pushed in and nearly drown. When we emerge, fighting for air, we don't want to see someone wading at the shallow end of the pool, wearing a casual smile and a perfectly fitting swimsuit, pretending to know what it took for us to break the water's surface, let alone take a single breath, applauding our bravery. I've poured out enough of my grief in public, on the page, in magazines, in bookstores, on television. I've seen people watch me carefully to see what I'll do as if I'm a test case of the ideal or perhaps failed "grieving mother."

I told the television journalist that Ronan's father had been good to him, but I left out the other truth, that he was not a good husband to me and I was not a good wife to him. In bookstores I gave readings and responded to audience questions, most of which I don't really answer: "How do you go on after such a loss?" "How do you cope?" My answer: "I have no idea." Writing, editing, book tours, interviews: all of this is a writer's *work*. It has little or nothing to do with bravery. Nobody is charging into warfare here. No gold stars are given because none are earned. I am no warrior of love or anything else. The one statement I repeat all the time when I'm asked these impossible questions is "I don't know anything definitive about anything, and neither do you." To askers' bewildered and disappointed faces, I can only say, "I'm alive. That's all I've got. You have to figure out how to live on your own."

As I delete these strangers' emails and dump their letters, which I've hardly skimmed, into the post office's tiny corner trash can—which is always overflowing with grocery ads, overdue bill warnings, catalogs for fishing gear and lingerie, and misrouted mail stamped RETURN TO SENDER—I think, *None of me or Kent or Ronan; none of us for you.* I feel strangely

proud of myself for choosing to let go of these connections, to create a boundary between my life and theirs. As a
woman with a disability, I've never been granted much privacy. People—especially strangers, are always asking questions: "What's wrong with you?" "What happened to your
leg?" "Why are you limping?" I always responded. I was
taught to be nice. As a result, I've struggled with knowing
whom to let in and whom to keep out, and this dilemma was
only intensified when Ronan was sick. "Nothing is as freeing
as grief" (Maggie Smith, "If Anyone Can Survive").

What I do know is that, apart from my female friendships,
which have so far outlasted every romantic relationship in
my life, and until Ronan and Kent, my connections with others were often projections of my own making and lacked
intimacy—and risk—as a result. So many "romances" were
letter-based (in other words, completely unreal, rooted in
fantasy, and therefore totally safe). I signed my effusive letters "yours" and "your Emily," but in truth I'd given very
little of myself, which is precisely the point of loving someone from a distance. I'd given only what I wanted to give and
in the privacy of my letter-writing mind. So I know the
power of a barrier between self and another.

Kent is the only other source of comfort. He is the planet
of stability and love and graciousness and physicality that I
orbit around. I can't imagine what I'd be doing without him.
I am not working; I have quit the job at the art school where
I taught literature and creative writing to kids who ranged
from wildly talented to woefully underprepared for college,
all of them desperate to make an impact, to matter. I so often

wanted to say, *I have nothing to offer you. Don't look to me for instruction of any kind.*

Now I'm perched in the church sanctuary each night when Kent gets home, where he often finds me shrouded in plumes of smoke, holding wads of crumpled newspaper and trying to make a fire in the stove—apart from the occasional space heater, it's the single source of heat in the building. "I knew how to do this when I was six!" I wail, but apparently now that I am an adult, the Girl Scout–level skill of starting a fire without setting off the smoke alarm is beyond my capabilities. I'm re-creating Kent's early bachelor life in this space, when he used to sit in a deck chair covered in a wool blanket and drink whiskey, huddled near the fire reading mysteries and crime novels.

At night we take long baths in the claw-foot tub in the solarium, with its starlit view and an angled architecture of skinny candles bending in odd directions from mismatched candelabras. It feels like we're resting in a constellation, rocked by the sky, the bright stars pinned overhead as if holding the darkness in place. Sometimes a draft of wind through a crack in the window shifts the wooden icon balanced on the tub's edge. Sometimes the rain falls loudly and steadily on the clear glass roof in a predictable rhythm; other times the sound pattern is erratic. I try to mark the beats with my fingers on my leg, on the tub's side, in the air. I love sitting in this room in the water against the body of this man. We smoke one cigarette each and drink one martini each, adding hot water again and again to the tub until we're ready to brave the cold of the unheated room and get out.

Kent asks me questions; I don't have a lot to say, and would prefer to listen to the rumble of his voice against my ear pressed to his chest. I splash my hand around in the water as if that's a form of conversation. I organize soft piles of bubbles so that my body is covered; I've never wanted to see it and I certainly don't want to see it now: this body that made a baby not fit for the world. This body that I have always carefully attended to and also despised. This body that, as my aunt announced to a roomful of people in a church basement at my grandmother's funeral lunch, was "made wrong." These are the unpleasant and impossible-to-resolve thoughts in my mind. I'm out of words and wearied by repeated attempts to call them forth. What I want most is to feel invisible, but also safe, which means being seen. It's confusing.

This life after Ronan's life ended is full of edges and triggers. I've been dropped from the jaws of dread, but I don't know what to do or feel when I'm not in the grip of waiting and watchfulness. It's like the first steep drop of a roller coaster that never levels out, the state of careening out of control, just goes on and on. I feel like an idiot (*idiot* isn't correct; more like a *monster*) to have ever talked about waiting for this "after" moment. I was sure I'd feel "relieved" when it was over (and I used that ridiculous word thousands of times), when Ronan was free of his physical suffering, free of a body incapable of living in this world. I am not relieved; I am haunted and full of a heavy misery that I thought would be easier to bear once his suffering was over. The great weight was supposed to be lifted, wasn't it? Now it feels as if it is just ramping up . . . but to what? The roller coaster creaks and crawls up the incline. The brutal ascent, again, of expectation.

The moment of Ronan's death was far worse than I expected, not knowing what or how to expect, despite all the therapy and support group sessions and the endless, endless talking, and this aftermath is worse than I anticipated as well. I can't stop imagining the crematory flames, the jump and whoosh as the door closes and Ronan's body disappears: inside the flame, inside the oven. During the day I close my eyes, trying not to see what I can't stop seeing. What happened to Ronan's tongue, his eyes, his toenails? I hear the roar of the fire in my dreams, feel it. Did they put his body in with a shovel, like something out of a horror movie? "What has the land done to your tongue?/It is not dirt I hear in your crumbling mouth./We did not bury you. When a tongue burns/is it burned always?/Does it hurt you?" (Maggie Smith, "Your Tongue").

My heart pounds as if I'm running uphill on a cold day, which I often do, powering myself up the steep hill behind the church, the cold slamming against my lungs as if someone is punching me, running to the edge of the mesa, where I feel the wind on my face and the sun on my head, inhaling dust and looking out over shrubs and desert mountains and sky sky sky, all of this beautiful sky and this ridiculously big and stupid world full of possibilities for everyone except my dead child, whom I will never see again, never touch or hold again. I want someone to explain to me what I've done wrong and strike me across the face.

I spent an entire year punching a heavy bag in the back

room of my Santa Fe rental house nearly every night, circling and bouncing on my toes, hitting and kicking until I couldn't feel my arms anymore and my right toe bled (*Tight is light*, I heard my coach say as I snapped my wrist back to my waist after a punch) and my eyes ran with sweat; now I want to *be* punched. I don't even need to be powered by Eminem's musical rage, as I once did; I'm creating my own, in my legs and my lungs. Once I'm back at the church I hammer out push-ups until I fall flat on the floor, listening to animals scurry across the roof.

I long for tangible, identifiable physical pain (burning lungs, sore legs, aching shoulders) as a kind of counterpoint to this mobile cloud of misery I inhabit, but I also long for comfort that simply eludes me. I shake Kent awake again in the middle of the night in a different house, our house, this church with its high ceilings and a resident ghost that only Kent's mother has ever seen ("Oh yes, she's friendly!" she told him years before she died).

"I should have gone to see Ronan. Don't you think I should have gone?" I lay my body across Kent's in the seamless darkness and he tells me that he insisted on seeing his mother's body at the funeral home after she died, and he's always regretted it. "It wasn't her," he says. His voice, thick with sleep, vibrates against my cheek, across my sore jaw. "And now that's my last image of her. You did the right thing. It's not Ronan. He's gone."

I ask Kent about cremation, as if he's an expert. What was the process like? Intimate? Detached? A mix of both? Did anybody touch Ronan or hold him moments before he was placed in the mouth of that fire? Did they look a final time at his face? I know that Dawn, a woman who loved Ronan and did bodywork for him, visited the funeral home and covered his body with rose petals. She must have said his name as she'd done when she massaged him with the small metal rollers she gripped lightly in her sun-spotted hands. But did anyone else know his name or say it out loud? "Do they use shovels? Are they big or little? Do they use their hands? Or a tool? Did they know his name? Do you think they said his name?" Kent doesn't know. (Years later, one of my best graduate students will reference a book written by a female mortician, the chapters precisely detailing the cremation process. I will look up the book online with the intention of ordering it. I never do.)

The questions, as well as the possible answers and the impossibility of the answers, make me retch into coffee cups, into the sink, in the shower. I want to crawl into pictures and hold my boy. I want to bolt out of my skin and into the air, into the dirt. This world holds and houses so much—why can't there be a space for my child in it? Dante's line from *The Divine Comedy* floats frequently in my head, like a thought tattoo: "I did not die, and yet I lost life's breath."

Oh, where was he? James Baldwin said, "Trust life, and it will teach you, in joy and sorrow, all you need to know." I had known both, so why did I still know nothing? Since my new home is rumored to be a friendly place for ghosts, I wait for Ronan's ghost to appear at the side of the bed, his scent of powder and prunes to float through the air. I listen for rattling chains, imagining myself in a melodrama I once watched as a child, when the ghost of a Victorian woman in a high-necked dress appeared near a washing machine at precisely 2:30 in the morning. Throughout my childhood I was bewitched and fascinated by that hour, often keeping myself up until 2:30, or lying awake in bed, pinned by fright into complete stillness, between 2:30 and 3:30, just to see if she'd appear, trembling with terror and anticipation, its own kind of perverse delight.

Meanwhile, the church in Madrid is our home, and I sit in the choir loft and look out over the small town—once a coal-mining town, then a ghost town, then a small, funky town of artists and veterans and social outliers, with a single paved main street. Dust floats up from the backs of trucks passing beneath the high window. Stray dogs roam the arroyo. Night creatures skitter in the belfry, and dust falls through the cracks in the hinged door to scatter over bills and half-written pages on the desk. If not kept indoors, cats don't last long against the bobcats and coyotes roaming freely over the hills. The brightly painted tourist shops turn various shades of blue and yellow and green in the changing light. Our neighbor's drunken arguments echo across the road. "I kicked you out! No, I kicked YOU out! FUCK YOU! No, FUCK YOU!" I can see people moving down Main Street as if I'm looking out over a miniature town of southwestern pioneers, only these are tourists buying turquoise and stone sculptures and bold statement necklaces made of braided leather and carefully polished bone.

I disrupt Kent's previously ultratidy home with my stacks of books and piles of vintage clothes and expensive night creams and messiness and erratic grief. I spend long hours in the sanctuary watching the embers from the morning fire flicker and die, listening to the wind chase dust and mice through the belfry and the occasional dull clang of the rusty bell creaking back and forth in the wind. I watch light change and deepen and organize itself into stripes and then squares as it moves across the wooden floors, marking the day's progress. Dust floats up and disappears in the air. I wait for something—anything—to happen. Nothing happens. I remember, from my early training in fire safety at Bible Camp, that embers are just as dangerous as flames, perhaps even more so, when it comes to sparking fire. Still: nothing.

If I'm not sitting in my house watching shadows and light scribble along the walls, I spend the afternoon driving around Santa Fe in willful, angry silence. I try to put the world on mute, because every song lyric is a trigger; every news sound bite or advertisement irritates me. If I could drive while keeping my eyes closed, I would, although the images I see inside my mind offer no comfort. Sooner or later I find an excuse to drive by the house where I lived with Ronan and his father and then with only Ronan, and imagine (then worry, then hope, then *demand* of who or what I don't know) that I will see myself walking through the front door, Ronan still alive and dressed for a walk (knitted puppy hat, neck support, abundant blankets around his sticklike legs). Maybe I'll glimpse myself in some alternative existence, the veil between this world and some other imagined world thinned to the point of transparency. I imagine myself as a character in a Dickens novel, the ghost of my own past, wonderfully plagued by impossible circumstance and visited often by the dead. Alternatively, I could be losing my mind, which hasn't been much of a safe space for some time, and now features a ticker tape of triggering thoughts.

Several times I park my car in front of the house and watch as the people who were my neighbors for two years and knew what was happening to my son, to my family, but never said a word to me—even on the morning of Ronan's death, when the funeral van with MORTUARY painted in white cursive letters on the door led a procession of commuters out of the cul-de-sac—shuffle in and out of their houses with gardening shears, yippy dogs on leashes, bags of groceries. I glare at them through the windshield and know they are glad I have moved on with my tragic kid and my broken life. Oh, I want to scream at them. I want them to see my face distorted by rage. I am more than ready for a fight, but most of them simply ignore me. I am angry with Ronan's father, but the thought of him also makes me want to weep. The day I left the house for good I threw our wedding album in the trash and hauled the heavy can out to the curb. I cannot locate an ounce of love for him, only a pity that spins quickly into anger. "You loved him once," my mother says. "He was a good man. This broke him." Was he? Did I? Is love really love if it doesn't last? Doesn't a child's death break everyone? Is this the excuse he uses to justify his rage? Is it the excuse I'm using to justify mine?

I am brimming; my senses are heightened and yet my body can scare up only ecstatic numbness. I am hungry all the time, but can only pick at food. Nothing tastes right; nothing sounds good. Birds fight for nest space in the just-budding trees, and I don't understand how this is happening. I wear the world on my finger like a thimble, tapping doors, testing the strength of dark windows that rattle in the early spring wind. Each day is a weapon: a couple unstrapping their dark helmets in a parking lot, a toddler brushing a stray curl from his forehead, a cloud in motion, light. My head is a balloon, a bomb, a gun. I have been ejected from the world of motherhood. As Nabokov once described it, I am living in "the poignant absurdity of the exile." Love has found me, and yet I am so lost.

I finger the tangle of Ronan's hair that's sealed inside a plastic bag. I am an unhinged lover, handling this dead hair from a dead boy, the missing beloved. The clipped points of his strands of hair look as small and light as feathers inside the thin plastic, too small even to press like a flower or a photo between the pages of an album or a memory book.

One day turns into the next. Spring deepens, the world warms. Now I drink too much, mindlessly smoke more than one cigarette, and want constant sex and attention. I want to be taken somewhere else, to travel outside thought and feeling, outside the body, freed from the mind and all its noisy, unlit corners. Instead I take naps and organize the china. I kill flies with my hands and leave them to shrivel on the windowsills, dark bodies that stir in a draft through a crack in the window, a false resurrection.

In *The Body Keeps the Score*, trauma specialist Bessel van der Kolk offers important insight into the physiological changes in the brain of a person who is experiencing trauma. Essentially, the parasympathetic nervous system gets frazzled. The body doesn't know where to look for a safe space of calm and comfort. Trauma causes people to continually be "bracing against and neutralizing unwanted sensory experiences." Enter: self-numbing. I've been here before: anorexia, exercise addiction, overspending, risky sexual behavior, drinking. All ways of dulling the "intolerable inner world" through behavior that provides a "false and paradoxical feeling of control." I know this, and yet I feel powerless. And guilty: I am alive. Ronan is not.

"You're freaking me out," Kent finally admits. Our fast and beautiful eight-month courtship feels as real to me as my own grief; it's the other half of my life that makes it a whole. But I feel erratic and sad and sometimes just . . . weird. I won't let him watch even half of a movie without trying to force his pants off, or crying uncontrollably for no reason at all. I worry I might lose him, too, which makes me even crazier, even needier. I am the speaker in this poem by Katie Ford, lamenting, "Love lays me on the rack/My desire's all gone wrong/It's starved/It's stupid, too, and strong."

So I venture out more, even though it is painful, trying to outmuscle the strength of whatever is driving me—and Kent—ragged. I run more, fast and hard and in all kinds of weather, until my right foot is numb and my prosthetic limb has rubbed raw sores around my crotch. I welcome the singular focus of the pain and don't try to heal the wounds; instead, I invite them, wincing at each step. I walk the short distance to the coffee shop in town, order a latte, and limp back, exhausted from the exchange of the most basic social pleasantries. A well-meaning person asks, "How are you?" In their eyes I see the real questions: *Your child died, why are you here, why aren't you screaming every hour of every day?* I respond with "I'm fine!" and feel as if I've swallowed an iron pipe.

Other times I walk farther. One afternoon I step into the parking lot of a local café, see a family, and stop moving as if I've been slapped. "I want to eat under the umbrella, Mama!" the little girl cries, although it is still too cold to do so. She is two, her brother I guess about five. Both have pale blond hair that curls up behind their ears as Ronan's did. Their parents are toned and tattooed, fit and young, a hip Santa Fe couple. They hold water bottles made of recyclable metal and the mother cleans the table with a disinfectant wipe before they all sit down. I rush across the parking lot before I can shout at them for being alive.

One morning I force myself to walk to town and smile at people I'm just beginning to know, but once in the coffee shop I am unable to sign the receipt for my latte. I hold the pen and start to write the "E" and then can do no more. The barista—who knows me from yoga class and who knew Ronan when I brought him here, motionless and soft in the front pack—notices what's happening, takes the slip, comps my coffee, and gives my hand a hard squeeze. The gentleness threatens to split me and I run out, too overwhelmed to even thank him for such a kindness.

On the path home I start thinking about all the death paperwork I filled out, asking the hospice nurse "Where do I sign?" and trying to remember the way it felt to write my name, and then after it: "mother." Sign *here* and *here* and *here*. I have written my last act as a mother. Now it seems I can write nothing at all, not even my name. I have also forgotten how to spell, and after a few "hey, are you okay?" return emails, where I realize all my misspellings, I stop writing these as well.

Eventually I stop going out, even when the weather gets warm enough for short sleeves and picnics and happy hours outside. I drink three French presses of coffee, one after the other, and then fall asleep for three hours. I am often up during the night, writing bad poetry on the chancel turned television room where an altar once stood, a muted crime drama on the screen, the violence rendered to the swipe and shadow of image: a girl silently hit by a car; a mute shoot-out on a city street; a fire in which not everybody escapes alive but their panicked mouths, opened wide, emit no sound. It's like trauma ballet—beautiful in gesture, terrible in content. I read translated haikus by Robert Hass, and this one in particular over and over again: "When it is bad/I go into the night/and the night eats me."

One night I crawl into Kent's lap and weep until my eyes are swollen and my throat is scratchy. "It's okay," he says, and rubs my back. Our therapist has recently asked us to do a horrible exercise in which we had to begin a sentence saying, "I hate it when you're . . ." We've just completed it. Kent said I was "needy." I said he was "distant." He said he's been in relationships with women who used crying as a form of manipulation, a way to win an argument. "I'm crying because I'm fucking SAD!" I wailed. I blubbered on about a song someone taught me as a child: "It's all right to cry, crying gets the mad out of you," but the mad and the madness won't leave me. I could cry for the rest of my life. I want him to be my "island of safety," as van der Kolk describes it, but I'm supposed to be able to find this island within my body, and yet my body has never been a safe space for me: not after amputation, not after Ronan's diagnosis, not after his death. Never.

But here, now, in this moment, we connect in our grief and our love, and in our still-new-lust-trust that feels both old and familiar, that feeling of comfort in the other's body, the other's presence, the other's promises. It is strange to watch someone die with another person. Somehow, you expect everyone will have died or is on the verge of death. But we lived. We are alive.

"I want to have a baby," I say, and it is maybe the truest thing I've ever said.

"Me, too," he replies.

Three hours later we wake up in the same position. The fire has gone out, and we are tangled in grief and the shared sweat of two bodies being pressed close together for a long time. The very picture, I can see now, of hope.

CHAPTER FIVE

El Fuego

Love is apart from all things.
Desire and excitement are nothing beside it.
It is not the body that finds love.
What leads us there is the body. . . .
Love lays hold of everything we know.

JACK GILBERT, FROM "THE GREAT FIRES"

Kent is out of town on assignment for a piece about the oil boom in North Dakota, so I've brought my friend Elizabeth to the doctor's office to find out if I'm actually pregnant.

"Do you think I imagined the positive test?" I ask her, adjusting my feet in the stirrups. "Like some kind of powerful wishful thinking?" I don't tell her that six weeks ago I took three tests before shaking Kent awake just as the sun was coming up to show him the fourth test and the two blue lines on the stick. "This is like a scene from a romantic comedy," I joked nervously as I placed the stick in his hands—carefully, as if it might break. "The middle aged woman telling her much older boyfriend she's pregnant, holding the proof, holding it out."

"Wow." His surprise was genuine. Our last round of intra-uterine insemination, followed by constant sex for two days straight, had been unsuccessful. This positive test was the result of our second round, and we'd committed to three rounds. "We did it," he said quietly, as if talking to himself.

"Strong swimmers," I said, and slapped him on the back. "Well done."

Moments before, as I was sitting in the unheated bathroom, no birds yet awake at that cold and early hour, the wind gently shaking the windows, my hands trembled as the results registered like a slowly developing photograph. I'd wanted another child since the moment Ronan was diagnosed, over two years earlier. That desire—profound, irrational, innate, and consuming—had been one small part of what shattered my marriage to Ronan's father. He resoundingly did not want another child.

But now I feel calm, and buzzing with excitement, fear, disbelief: in short, amazement. Those two parallel blue lines, again and again, on test after test, felt like a curse being lifted, the promise of a second chance. The slog and terror and horror of the last two years still hangs like a visible banner in the sky, but now perhaps there will be a new one to join it—one that flutters with a different story, carries a new and more hopeful message, one that suggests beginnings instead of endings. Is it possible? Could these two realities exist simultaneously?

"I'm sure you're prego," Elizabeth says, flipping through a magazine. "Those things are super accurate."

I look at her. She grins. "You have no idea what you're talking about," I say.

"Absolutely no clue."

Just as I begin to laugh, the curtain rattles open, signaling the doctor's entrance. My heart lifts into my throat and my hands make damp prints on the paper "gown" over my lower half. I've been in so many doctors' offices, for so many things, for so much of my life, but this is different. This is a fertility clinic, a place that I, like so many of the other patients here, never expected to enter. My first visit to these beige, overly air-conditioned offices in the basement of an Albuquerque hospital was with Ronan's father when our son was still alive. We sat across the desk from the doctor, listening to the genetic testing we'd need to do after all the IVF steps to be sure that any viable embryos that may or may not become viable fetuses that may or may not become healthy children wouldn't have Tay-Sachs and wouldn't die the way Ronan was dying. The entire procedure would be massively expensive, invasive, time-consuming, and nerve-racking. On the drive back to Santa Fe, my then husband finally said, "I can't do this." I understand this now, but then I was furious, feeling strongly that he'd betrayed me in the worst possible way. What kind of man (or woman) denies the other the possibility of a child, especially when facing the death of another? I screamed at him, refused to speak to him, punished him in every way I knew how, as if that would win him over—in retrospect, an obviously faulty strategy. I wanted another child so much that I was more than willing to burn down our relationship to get it, which is exactly what I did.

"What do we have here?" the doctor says as he washes his hands. This is my least favorite medical greeting and makes me bristle with annoyance. Do doctors actually believe this is a comforting thing to say? Nobody likes to feel like a science experiment, and it's clear to any patient who isn't a casual observer that doctors are coached to engage in "chatty small talk" while washing their hands. Perhaps this makes it more likely that when they do turn around, they will see a person and not just a patient. (Years later, when I'm speaking with my friend Lucy, a doctor, during grand rounds at Cedars-Sinai Medical Center in Los Angeles, where Ronan was born, she will turn to me just before our presentation and whisper, "Saying 'patients are people' will blow most doctors' minds.") Elizabeth squeezes my shoulder as the doctor starts flipping through my chart, his eyes watering behind the thick lenses of his glasses.

"Hmmmm. Uh-huh," he mutters. I feel my body go hot with annoyance and terror.

After Ronan's father and I officially separated and were living apart, I returned to this fertility clinic alone and maxed out a credit card to buy expensive vials of donor sperm. I chose the "genetic material" of a Cuban college student who claimed to be good at math and whose blood was triple-tested for the Tay-Sachs gene, a literal teenager who marked the box indicating that a potential child would be allowed to contact him in the future if he or she so desired. I booked my appointments on the pink master fertility calendar and took home the instructional DVD, which came in a nondescript case with no identifying information, as if to avoid advertising the content. I thought of the *Playboy* magazines wrapped in brown paper that my mother once found in my brother's room and that prompted a "family meeting," which also involved a horrifying demonstration of a banana and a condom that made my brother and me both want to melt into the floor with embarrassment.

One night after Ronan was asleep, I poured myself a large globe of Merlot and sat on the couch to watch the DVD. A woman with feathered brown hair sat behind a desk, carefully and patiently opened each syringe, and explained how to administer the shots and what they would do. It was like an infomercial, but without any flashy advertising, poor production quality, and a woman who looked and spoke like a very bored robot. After listening to her deliberately emotionless voice describe the protocol for fifteen minutes, I slammed the computer shut. It was nearing the end of winter, and the world beyond the window was colorless and bleak, the trees empty of leaves, or buds, or any physical signs of hope or changing seasons. The bright moon only called attention to the spindly trees, the lack of life. Everything felt like it might crumble or crack at the lightest touch.

I settled into the air mattress next to Ronan's crib and wept. After all it had cost me, I wanted another child, but not enough to do it by myself. How would I manage time and money? I knew so many women who had done this successfully, but I didn't think I could be one of them. I wasn't wealthy. I didn't have a trust fund or family members in a position to assist me financially. I had student loans and other debt. I wanted to live a creative life; since the age of fourteen I'd been working two or more jobs at once and I knew how hard that was, and the energy that would likely not be left over for single motherhood. How would I manage life with a "normal" child? Had this experience of parenting made it impossible for me to be "good" at it, whatever that meant?

Soon after I met Kent, I knew I wanted to parent with him. I loved him, yes, but he was also clearly a natural father who had not yet been given the chance to see how deeply the role would suit him; who had been told, falsely, that he wouldn't be good at it, a belief he had been dragging around like a curse for almost thirty years. The things we say to each other carry enormous power; when they're meant to wound, when they're not, or even when they're said under the breath of a doctor in the exam room.

"Okay," the doctor finally says, and looks in my direction. Sort of. This isn't the fertility doctor I know well, the younger guy from Texas who wears cowboy boots and asks me about writing and treats me with compassion and has so many kids that he and his wife both drive large vans to shuttle them between school and their various activities. His office is covered in school pictures as well as candid shots of these beautiful children, family photos at Disneyland, a pyramid of kids on top of a mountain, individual shots of each towheaded cutie on horseback. We've talked about my advanced maternal age, my divorce, my book, and Ronan, whom he remembers by name and always asks about. I was a patient with a husband and a child; then a patient who was newly single, grieving, and childless; and now a patient with a boyfriend twenty years my senior—all of these patients trying to get pregnant, all of them, in different ways, bereaved. All of them hopeful, even if that hope was just a momentary flicker, easily mistaken for a trick of the light.

This doctor—tall and bald, with age-spotted hands—is still flipping through my chart. He has not yet, and never will, ask for my name.

"Huh," he says yet again, in a voice you might use to brush a dead fly from a windowsill, and then, in a deeper voice, "Ohhh." Elizabeth shoots me a look.

I sit up on my elbows. "What is it?" Did "my" doctor make a note? And is this guy going to tell me what it is? I like doctors and have always trusted them innately, usually without negative consequences. The surgeon who performed all of my orthopedic surgeries is one of the kindest men I've ever known; he has enabled me to have the life I do, and I respect and admire him. I email him occasionally to check in and sometimes we share funny cat videos. I've spoken alongside him at medical conferences. Even when I was a child, he talked to me respectfully and always told me the truth about what was happening to me, from losing a foot to having a hip modification surgery. I trusted him with my body and my life. I still would.

This doctor raises a finger to silence me, presumably. Elizabeth licks her lips and looks at the floor; I can see she's getting angry.

"You have Tay-Sachs?" he asks without looking up. My legs are straining a bit in the stirrups, the muscles of my inner thighs beginning to tremble. I can feel the lip of my prosthesis digging into my bottom rib.

Now I'm angry. "If I had Tay-Sachs, I'd be dead," I say as calmly as I can. "I'm a carrier. My son had Tay-Sachs and he died." I can almost anticipate the next question, but still feel slightly surprised when he asks it.

"You must be Jewish."

"I'm not."

"But you have Tay-Sachs. That's a Jewish disease."

"I do not." My face is hot; my heartbeat is wonky and frantic. "It is not."

"So you're not Jewish." He *whispers* this, but I feel like he's just shouted *"You're a Jew!"*

"She's not," Elizabeth interrupts loudly, "but I am. You can't get it just by being in the same room with us." I've brought the right friend: my outspoken, New York City born and bred *Jewish* friend, who will leap to my grateful defense. When people used to stare at Ronan when we were all out for dinner she'd shout, *"What are you looking at? Mind your own business!"*

The doctor isn't listening, but he continues to read and, looking confused, flips through the file and says, "Ah, I see. Your son died."

"That's correct," I stammer, and then, "He did. His name was Ronan." This last part he clearly doesn't hear, or else chooses to ignore.

"Ronan," Elizabeth repeats loudly. Her voice cracks a bit.

The doctor tosses the file on the counter, wiggles his big hands into a pair of blue latex gloves, and with about as much preamble as you would use to check the oil level in your car, says, "Open up." He is not gentle with the probe, and he doesn't tell me what he's about to do or what he'll be looking for. I'm trying to remember what it felt like when my Los Angeles doctor searched for Ronan's embryonic form to confirm my first pregnancy, in 2009, but imagining my lost boy as a microscopic cluster of already doomed cells when he's now so *gone* after living so briefly and painfully is visibly upsetting me. Elizabeth grabs my hand while the doctor digs around in my uterus. "Turn the screen so she can see it," she demands, and he does, without acknowledging either one of us.

"There's a fetal pole," he says, "but nothing else. No heartbeat." The only noticeable sounds are the paper gown crinkling as I shift, the muted voices outside the door, a nervous laugh trailing down the hallway, the hum of a photocopier on the other side of the wall.

"I think it's exactly six weeks today," I say, embarrassed by my shaking voice. "It could be too soon to see anything." I don't want to admit that I've googled this fact on a variety of medical websites. I don't realize until this moment how much I want to be pregnant. Kent and I had weighed the pros and cons of beginning this journey, a word I hate but that we keep saying aloud—as in *the parenting journey*. We wanted a child, yes, but there were many factors to consider: our combined ages (ninety-eight), the length of time we'd been together (not quite a year), the uncertainty of our careers.

Doctor Zero Bedside Manner slides out the probe, scoots across the floor on his wheeled stool, snaps off his latex gloves, tosses them in the trash, and starts scribbling in my file with an expensive-looking pen. Without looking up, he says, "We'll test your HCG levels now and monitor them for the next few days, but it looks like a no-go. We'll see you again if you decide to try again." And with that, he stands up and leaves the room.

"A no-go?" Elizabeth gushes. "What in the actual fuck!"

She helps me off the table and I dress silently. It is only after my blood has been drawn on a different floor and I'm in the elevator pressing the gauze into my oozing arm that I burst into tears. Elizabeth is fuming, her face practically shaking. "I hate that fucking guy," she says, and then she's crying, too. We go up and down in the carriage for a few minutes. I sob on Elizabeth's shoulder as we move between floors; people get in and out of the elevator without saying a word. I could wax on about the "parenting journey" all I wanted, but the truth was this: I wanted a baby. I wanted to be a mom who saw her child grow and live. I never thought of it as replacing Ronan, although some would later accuse me of this. The myth of the "replacement child." Creating life is and was a primal instinct, and one that has felt and will always feel completely beyond any intellectualizing or mental control.

Many of my friends know I have been trying to get pregnant, and I call them on the drive back to Madrid after I drop Elizabeth off at her apartment, my car winding through the scrubby desert ringed by mountains, surfing through the shifting shadows that change with each curve and slant of light, speeding past the man in Golden who has a collection of maybe a thousand glass bottles on his lawn and who always stops to wave at cars as they pass by. I call my lesbian friends, who have been so helpful as I gathered information about donor sperm and IVF, and who have openly shared the steps they took to have children. I call my friend Kate, who struggled to get pregnant and will eventually work as the executive director of a nonprofit that supports families seeking fertility treatments and resources, while working to erase the stigma concerning what some still see as "artificial" intervention via science and technology. Finally I call Kent. He's at an Applebee's in Dickinson, he tells me, the town's finest dining establishment, drinking his second glass of terrible wine and working his way through a salty Caesar salad. The sound of his voice is like a balm.

"We'll try again," he says, but I hear in his voice the helplessness and disappointment that mirrors my own. "I'll be home tomorrow," he says, "and we can start right away."

He laughs, which makes me laugh. I say, "Remember when you asked me out and when I told you which day I was free you said you had to finish building the deck?" He had called me at my office at the college, and I'd thought, *Hmmm, finishing your deck over time with the woman you're supposedly wooing. No way, dude.* "You can see me tonight or next week," I said. "Okay, tonight," he responded. "The deck can wait.

"Yeah, yeah," he says. "You love that story. But I didn't work on the deck, remember?"

He didn't. We went to dinner (spicy curry and red wine at an Indian restaurant in an adobe building downtown), and then tried to go to a bar. When we stepped out of the car he slipped his hand in mine, and this felt so right that we didn't even care that the bouncer at Santa Fe's hippest watering hole decided we didn't pass muster. Too old and "uncool," I guess. We shrugged, although I was feeling sixteen and awesome. We took a flask of mescal into the Black Forest campground outside Santa Fe, and quickly steamed up the windows of Kent's Volvo. We were both so quick to get out of our seatbelts that I think our first kiss was more like a collision of teeth. In the back of the car he kicked me with his boot— "ooh, sorry, baby"—and we finally tumbled out onto a patch of dirt, he took off his shirt, spread it on the ground, and we made love under the moon as bright as a spotlight, erasing any visible twinkling of stars. The next day he called and said, "My shirt smells like pinecones and pussy."

With Kent, I felt good and sexy and *happy,* which felt strange at first, and then like a great relief with a strong and acidic chaser of survivor's guilt and disbelief. Paolo Bacigalupi, from *The Drowned Cities*: "The problem with surviving was that you ended up with the ghosts of everyone you'd ever left behind riding on your shoulders." What messages or warnings might these ghosts have? I didn't feel like my "old self," but I did feel different. Both old and new at once. The ghosts would never leave me, and frankly, the expectation that they might—another way of subscribing to this silly notion that "time heals all wounds"—didn't resonate. Time doesn't heal anything; it just changes things—reshapes and reorients them. This simultaneity was strange and disorienting, wonderful and frightening. I felt easier, somehow, although my life did not, and it would become even more complicated in the upcoming months, as Ronan's condition worsened. Kent accepted that. I could scarcely believe it.

A few dates later, Kent said. "I want to be a couple with you." A straightforward expression of desire. I was surprised, but also glad for it. I didn't think I'd ever date again, let alone find love. I didn't trust anyone or anything. I shouldn't feel happy, either, I reasoned, not when I was going to lose my kid, who never got to live any kind of decent life.

"My life is very complicated," I said, a fact so obvious I felt ridiculous and embarrassed as soon as I said it aloud.

"So it's a fair question," he responded. Ronan was sleeping in his crib, the only time he ever seemed at peace and undisturbed, and Kent and I were sitting in my home office after having rolled around on an air mattress. The hot summer light made his blue eyes brighter, the different colors in his hair—gray, brown, black, red—more pronounced.

It seemed so outrageous, and yet so right, that I agreed.

When Kent and I returned to the fertility clinic a week later, anticipating that I would need to have a D & C, in the same room but now with the kind and familiar doctor from Texas, we heard the heart of the embryo that would become Charlie beating out a fast rhythm.

"There it is," the doctor said in his Texas twang, which suddenly felt like the most beautiful sound in the world next to the heartbeat. "Nice and strong."

Kent looked like he might faint. He was speechless, which is very unlike him. "Congratulations, you two," the doctor said, and shook both of our hands.

"Not what I expected him to say," Kent finally said when the doctor left.

I, too, was dumbstruck. I felt wonder like a warmth rising up in my body, even though I was shivering in the cold exam room.

A few months later, when Kent and I saw the tiny shadow that would become Charlie's capable, strong body on the large ultrasound screen, I thought of Ronan's lost, powerless body. There on the massive screen was a living child rubbing her eyes in funky 4D images that made her look like she was lounging in some kind of bumpy uterus moon crater. I half expected an embryonic astronaut to float through that black space on a nonumbilical cord and plant a flag near her head. All of her limbs were accounted for, her DNA triple-checked for Tay-Sachs and cleared. The chambers of her heart had been measured and observed, her brain examined from above for any potential problems. Her heart was beating out her living, wombed time in the dark and quiet room, a fast, insistent drumbeat. The vibrating inkblots on the screen were explained to us: "That's the blood moving in and out of her heart, that's her kidney, that's her bladder."

The last time I had been this close to a child, I had been washing his dead body, although I had to carve those images from imagination alone because I had no visceral memory of them. Did I do that? I can picture myself leaning over Ronan's still body in the blue tub, washing his hair, weeping—or is this a stock image that I'd planted there? Did my mother do this labor? Ronan's cold forehead, his skeletal limbs, his perfect feet that pointed toward but never fully touched the ground.

"You're so fearless and brave, having another baby," a lot of people gushed when I announced I was pregnant, as if my experience with Ronan would forever swear me off having another child; as if I would be overcome with worry about what might happen to him or her. But as Gloria Steinem correctly observed, "the myth of the fearless choice" is matched by the myth of the phoenix rising from the site of destruction and chaos, spreading its glorious and colorful wings. People do what they must do.

"Wow," Kent said, and his eyes literally widened. I, too, felt electrified by a mix of surprise and elation; I know better than most people that everything is built to wreck. But this was also true: the anchor on this ship had dropped. I wasn't nearly as fearful as I expected. The worst had already happened. Somehow this increased my tolerance for risk and not the other way around.

That summer Kent continued to cut boards in his woodshop and build and paint the wooden deck on the north side of the church, with its view of the mesa and the sage-spotted hills beyond. I liked to watch him walk up to the house from the workshop, a bandanna around his head, a tool belt around his waist, heavy with tools, a piece of the deck held in his big hands. When the deck was finished, we had dinner parties there, and many long talks about our future.

After I got pregnant and before Kent and I were married, I liked to sit on the west-facing deck and read. My concentration, which had been focused to a fine point while Ronan was living, and then, after his death, fractured by the finality of loss that scattered all organized thought, was slowly emerging again. I found solace—as I always have—in novels, poetry, nonfiction. I wasn't triggered by every scene with a child or even a casual mention of motherhood, and I started reviewing books again, writing again, spelling words correctly again. I thought about the baby we would have, anticipating picnics on this deck, and then a toddler learning to walk by clinging to the posts freshly painted a gentle blue. It appeared that I was getting a second chance. I felt tethered to the world in a way I'd never felt before, matched by alternating waves of panic that were often so fierce I had to sit down. A new life of motherhood was beginning, but leaving that other mother—Ronan's mother—behind meant leaving my son behind as well, and that I would and could not do. If our struggle as son and mother formed the anchor to a more difficult time in my life, this boat was staying put.

On the Fourth of July holiday, a friend snapped a candid photograph of Kent and me. Because Charlie is a secret in this captured moment, known only to us, it is our first photo as parents. We're at a baseball game for the local Santa Fe team, Fuego, sitting side by side in the bleachers, and we are laughing. We haven't told anyone we're pregnant, but if you look closely you can see that we're holding knowledge we alone share: a secret born of love, and the child, not visible yet, who would shape—and seal—our lives together.

A girl who would live her own life. Create a new fire.

CHAPTER SIX

Spring

Speckled egg, brown egg, or sky blue with black marks—

Having broken once, the world re-forms
in miniature.
Over and over, in the nest
between two limbs; in the hollow of grass
at a marsh edge.

It's relentless, the way it keeps trying
to return.
Joy
Joy
Joy

JENNY GEORGE, "SPRING"

Kent and I are about to have a child, a girl. Together we're just a bit younger than the hundred-year-old church where we live, and where Kent had been living alone since 1996. We cut and stack wood in the basement and haul it up in sturdy canvas bags for the wood-burning stoves. I love this task, even when I'm hugely pregnant, as it reminds me of the books about "frontier women" that I read voraciously as a kid growing up in Wyoming.

The church's ceiling is seventeen feet high. The foundation is sinking slightly, which means when the dip in the floor of the altar begins to look like it's actually sinking, Kent puts on a mask that looks straight out of World War I trench warfare, crawls under the house ("What, like through a *tunnel?*" I ask him. "Of course!" he replies), and pushes the floor up while I stand just outside the room's edge, my eye on the floor, bellowing, "Okay, it's going up!" as loudly as I can.

Like most residents of Madrid, we have a recurring mouse problem. A pack rat the size of a small cat is building what looks like a two-story critter condo in the basement, complete with torn-up blankets for a bed and little bits of food stashed in the corners. We wash dishes in a large silver bowl that sits in the sink and toss the water out onto the lawn. The choir loft overlooks the main room of the sanctuary; Kent built a separate bedroom five years earlier and converted the altar into a den with a television on one wall. I dutifully ride the elliptical machine in the corner for an hour every day. In other words, there's no designated place for a nursery.

Up until the arrival of a clothes-and-beauty-products-obsessed fiancée and a newborn, the church had a rugged and sexy "ultimate bachelor pad" air, which Kent used repeatedly to his advantage. So many women fell for the line *Hey, baby. Ever slept on an altar?* although its success was possibly helped along by his tight leather pants and long braid. The place certainly felt dreamy when the two of us sat in a hot, fragrant tub for hours before running into the icy bedroom and sleeping naked to transfer body heat, but now dangers for a baby loom in every corner: the church has no insulation; one of the cabinets in the small kitchen has been leaning forward since 1996 (later, we will discover that a surprisingly sturdy hand mixer has been holding it up for decades); the only sources of heat are two wood-burning stoves, and the particulates in smoke are unsafe for a tiny person's lungs. The "kitchen," out of which Kent has produced five-course meals for groups of fifteen or more people for over twenty years, was once the vestry for the priest, who served this church (the building itself was never consecrated) and other small congregations along the Turquoise Trail connecting Santa Fe and Taos through the 1950s. About as big as two large closets lined up end to end, the kitchen reminds me of the narrow room where as a child I met my dad after church—as he was hanging up his clerical robe and his heavy cross—and told him to "hurry up, I'm starving, your sermon was too long and we want pancakes."

For this space to be suitable to have a *baby* living here, there's much to do. I've spent the last eight-plus months calling and scheduling local contractors; taking bids on new windows and deliberating insulation strategies; picking out kitchen tiles; choosing paint swatches for the new windows. We are planning to tear down the kitchen-vestry and rebuild the whole thing, and so there is jackhammering and digging and, at some point, a shirtless worker, the son of a neighbor, throwing stones off the roof and grunting, reminding me of the Thundarr the Barbarian cartoons I used to watch when my parents slept in on Saturday mornings.

One afternoon, as I'm lying down to relieve my aching back, thinking, *Being pregnant at thirty-nine is a whole different ball game than it was at thirty-four*, I sense that the baby is not moving as much as usual; it's calm in there, too calm. Charlie is a kicker, a twister; the print of her hand often crosses my stomach like she's dancing a form of fetal Zumba. I call the doctor, who says it's better to come in than to lie awake worrying. *Better safe than sorry*, that old line that works on me every time, especially given that I am the oldest mother at the women's clinic where I go once a week for check-ins. At my "advanced maternal age," an indisputable fact scrawled across the top of all of my charts with a black Sharpie, I could easily be the mother of some of the mothers waiting to see my doctor. I scan their birth dates when I sign in: 1992, 1994, 1997.

Just before midnight, Kent and I get into the truck and bump along the winding country road to the hospital in Albuquerque, a trip that takes a little over an hour. And then we wait. After we've both fallen asleep under the white, buzzing lights of the exam room, a friendly intern finally arrives to assess the situation.

"Okay." She gestures for me to scoot down to the end of the table after I've told her about the decreased motion. "Big reach," she warns, and she's not kidding. I wouldn't be surprised if her hand touches the top of Charlie's head. She gropes for a minute, and then lets me know I have signs of early labor. As I had with Ronan, I have already scheduled a C-section; without the ability to push down with both feet equally during the labor process, I might shift the positioning of my hips and affect my mobility. Charlie's birth is scheduled for March 10, only four days away and already a bit shy of the recommended thirty-nine-week mark, so the intern gives me a labor-stopping drug. "Great," I say without question, and swallow the big white pill.

The medication doesn't just stop labor, it induces a pre-scribed and apparently totally legal hallucinogenic trip. Twenty minutes along the dark road through the mountains, I start singing "The Long and Winding Road" and giggling. I am totally high and loving every moment of it.

Kent looks confused and slightly bemused, but when he checks the gas gauge, his face registers alarm. "Fuck!" he shouts. "We have no gas." He lifts his hands.

"I love your hands," I murmur, pawing at them. They look strong, long, and manly. "Hands!" I shout.

"Seriously," he says, swatting me away. "Stop it. We have no gas."

"Oh, that's not a problem," I say. "It will be daylight soon, and we can just wait along the side of the road until the sun comes up and someone comes along. It's like being in a West-ern! Fun!"

"Wait on the side of the road? Yeah, no."

At this point, I can no longer see anything but what appear to be constellations of very bright and evenly spaced stars across the black dome of my vision, as if I've been on the receiving end of a knockout punch but am still awake.

"All the stations are closed," Kent mumbles, pulling into one Chevron, and then, just as quickly, pulling out again.

"Geronimo!" I yell and loosen my seatbelt. "Ooh, I'm dizzy," I say. "I need to feel free."

"Put that back on," he says. "What did they give you?"

"Something amazing," I say. "Although, it's so weird. I can't really see."

"What do you mean you can't see? Jesus," Kent replies, and I can hear him nervously tapping the wheel.

"Well, I can see stars and bright lights," I say. "A little universe that's all mine."

"Right," he says, reaching around me to clip the seatbelt back over my belly. "We're going to drive to the last hill and then coast. We're gonna make it. Just . . . look at the lights, I guess, and try to relax."

"COOL!" I shout. "It's like the movie *Titanic*!" I turn to him: "Jack! I trust you!"

"Oh god," Kent says. "That's such a terrible movie."

We do just that. We coast. We roll past the houses on the edge of Madrid: the sculptor's shed on the left side of the highway; the yard full of ten-foot iron sculptures of human forms and horses and abstract shapes; the dirt yard on the right side littered with wood scraps and truck parts and a few iron skeletons of cars propped up on blocks. We pull into the driveway just as the car goes kaput.

"Don't ever tell your mom I ran out of gas when you were pregnant," Kent says, setting his forehead on the wheel with relief. He gets me up to bed and I sing a few more nonsensical songs before falling asleep for twelve hours.

The next morning brings an out-of-season snowstorm in Madrid and Santa Fe that feels equal parts winter and spring. A light, wet snow falls and smells like rain, with long spaces between the falling flakes. I'm feeling restless, the baby is spinning to her own baby beatbox soundtrack, and after Kent pours a can of gas into the tank that will take me to the nearest station, in Lone Butte, for a proper refill, I decide to go into town to pick up a ski sled that's been offered to me by one of Kent's former colleagues. It will allow us to ski and pull Charlie behind us. I can't quite imagine ever doing this, but it's such a generous gift that I accept.

March is, by nature, a mercurial month in most parts of the Northern Hemisphere, an odd stretch of time awkwardly stitching together the seasons of winter and spring, but driving through Santa Fe I feel edgier than I'd like to, and the weather grows increasingly strange, suggesting some larger, more epic unpredictability. The sky feels as though it has dropped lower; in New Mexico it usually feels high and endless and wide. I realize I'm driving hunched over, as if I need to duck when I pass beneath trees lightly coated in snow. On the way to pick up the sled, I pass the entrance to the Upaya Zen Center, where I did a long weekend of "mindfulness and death training" before Ronan died. I feel a catch in my throat, like the bile that rose when I once got turned around and by mistake drove past the Santa Fe crematorium where Ronan's body was prepared and of course burned, and I just got the car door open before I barfed.

I load the sled into the back of the truck and the sky drops another level, seems even darker, and now the snow is falling fast and wet, like heavy white rain. The whole world feels nervous.

When I get home, I start painting the trim of the new window a green color that's just a few shades darker than a pea and that blends in nicely with the cream walls. But I keep redoing the same strip of wood and then forgetting and starting again. I feel scattered, my brain at half-mast. I also have a sudden and very out-of-character impulse to organize drawers. "Yeah, that is definitely weird," Kent says when I tell him. I go into the bedroom, fuss about with a sock drawer, read a few birthday cards that have gotten lodged in the back, and finally lie down. After a few minutes Kent comes in to lie down beside me. "It's weird out," he observes.

"I just wish my water would actually break so I'd know that she was on the way," I say into his forearm.

Remarkably, as soon as the words are out of my mouth, as if my body is obeying a command, my water literally breaks. Kent is not convinced.

"Are you sure? That seems a bit odd."

I agree that it's like a terribly coincidental moment from a dopey romantic comedy. "But there is water," I say, "or fluid, I guess. Or else I wet my pants."

"Are you sure? We were up all night last night. Maybe you just wet your pants. That makes more sense."

"Maybe." My water never broke with Ronan; he was right on time for his C-section, down to the minute.

"I'll just go take a shower and then let's see what happens, okay?" Kent says.

A few minutes later, I walk into the bathroom trailing puddles of amniotic fluid behind me and announce, "We've gotta go." I've never seen Kent get dressed so fast. The storm has passed; the wet spring snow melted quickly, and although the roads through the mountains shine in the darkness, they aren't slippery, and we make it to the hospital in record time.

My doctor is not on call, so six hours later, Charlie is delivered by two young doctors who, in Kent's words, "look as if they graduated from high school yesterday." After they speak with me about what to expect during the procedure— a speech they've clearly memorized carefully—they leave the room and I burst into tears. The nurse sends in the attending physician, who assures me that she's done "thousands" of C-sections.

The operation is harrowing in the way all operations are, when you have placed your life (and in this case, the baby's, too), in another person's hands, but this C-section goes on twice as long as the first, with lots of blood spatters on the sterile screen between my head and my belly, and more pushing and pulling than I remember with Ronan. I finally hear that "I'm in the world now" wail-roar, the beginning of life, and Kent is with the baby and they are swaddling her in a blanket, and then they are bringing her to me and she is alive and screaming.

Our girl is a redhead, or more of an orange head as it's still just fuzz, and she is in my arms. Someone takes a photograph of me with her and I see it, sent to me via text on my hourly "ambulation" around the ward to discourage post-op blood clotting. I stop walking and stare at the photo as if it's someone else's body, baby, and life, which is just the way I often felt on mornings with Ronan.

How can this be? I think, as I often thought then. I can hardly believe Ronan is dead; I can hardly believe Charlie is alive. I'm overcome with sensory images of the births of the boy and the girl as I stand in the corridor trembling: with relief, with sadness, lost in the magnificent float of painkillers. I close my eyes and experience what feels like a gravitational pull into the orbits of both children, the memories tangled and jumbled and crossed until I can't remember with which birth they align: thick chocolate chip cookies delivered every afternoon at Cedars-Sinai in Los Angeles; a dramatic blood splatter against the blue screen during the procedure in Albuquerque, followed by the anesthesiologist asking me purposefully distracting questions about my favorite books; the harsh chill of the room; a boy on a scale, his fists in the air; a girl in a soft pink blanket, her nose gently sloped; the white hats and clear bassinets of newborns; thick maxi pads taped over the belly scars; the tug of lips on the nipple and the rush of hormones that comes with the letdown of breast milk. To whom do they belong, these images? Which child? Which mother? Which world?

The shuffle and chatter of nurses at their station, the curl of laughter from a room where a visitor has just been welcomed, the crinkling sound of someone holding flowers wrapped in stiff plastic moving past me—within the midst of this medical orbit, in this collision of sensory images, I feel as if the boundary between the worlds of past and present have thinned and I'm somehow holding both children at once. It's a feeling I will have over and over again. As it's happening I think, *Remember this,* but it's a pointless instruction. The body never forgets.

In *The Body Keeps the Score,* Bessel van der Kolk writes: "We now know that trauma compromises the brain area that communicates the physical, embodied feeling of being alive. These changes explain why traumatized individuals become hypervigilant to threat at the expense of spontaneously engaging in their day-to-day lives." I am reminded of how the body holds memory, or what van der Kolk describes as "actual changes in the brain," three days after Charlie's birth, when we are released from the hospital and travel to Eldorado, a town just outside Santa Fe, where we stay at our friends Nancy and Libby's house until the still-being-installed heating system in the church is up and running. My parents join us, sleeping in the study and holding Charlie as much as possible.

Kent and I sleep in the guest bed with Charlie on her back between us. In the hospital, when she wasn't nursing, which she took to like a pro, just as Ronan had, she slept best with me, out of the clear-sided box of her hospital bassinet. (This will remain true, earning her the nickname Barnacle Bell, as she will not sleep unless pressed up close to a body.) The nurses and doctors advised against co-sleeping (as do all the parenting books I read through before I had Ronan, all of which I've since thrown out). But I ignored them; I wanted to feel her body next to mine. Now, released into this cocoon of a warmly decorated room, I feel tired, but also weirdly vigilant in a way I never was while pregnant. Ronan had been safe in my body, or partially safe; it was his entrance into the world that started the short, brutal clock of his life ticking away.

I've always found the transition away from a hospital awkward, in part because I find bright white rooms and corridors with the occasional bad painting or distracting decoration—a paper heart, a Santa cutout, a pumpkin, depending on the season—hugely comforting. Hospital nightlife has appealed to me, since childhood. I love the novelty of a loud ringing phone in the middle of the night and other ambient noises, like the clatter of wheels across tile floors, the low voices of doctors and nurses, the occasional laugh or a *shhhh*, the blaring lights that show all the corners and all the potential places from which danger might unexpectedly emerge.

Being able to see everything made me feel safe. As a child I insisted that I sleep directly under the brightest light, so I could "see all the corners." In the hospital I always felt nothing could happen to me since the entire building was filled with people whose job it was to guard the bodies in their care. It feels good, but also odd to be in Eldorado, where the quiet is punctured only by the occasional howl of a coyote or the sound of my mom loading the dishwasher in Nancy and Libby's kitchen.

March remains a mercurial month, warm edging toward hot during the day, but still dropping into the forties at night. The sky is momentarily streaked with sunlight, and then very quickly dark. A warm breeze is followed by a chilly one. Sun shines over one part of the desert, and a cloud threatens in the other, like fighters squaring off in the ring. The moon is a bright lamp. I keep a palm spread across Charlie's chest, just to check, just to be sure, just to know, and then just to double-check again, to know again.

Around two in the morning I am still staring at the moon—has it transitioned to a brighter shade of white? Or blue? A different shape? Are my thoughts frazzling *again*? I don't want to return to the mania I experienced during Ronan's illness: up all night with ideas rolling out unstoppably, unable to sleep for days at a time. Kent, exhausted from two nights of fitful sleep on the slab of a hospital cot, is sleeping flat on his back and hasn't moved for hours. Then I hear a strange but also familiar sound: a low, strained rattling, and it's coming from Charlie. I sit straight up in bed and shout Kent's name. He bolts up and immediately puts his hand on the baby. "She can't breathe," I say, barely getting the words out. "She can't breathe." All the blood leaves Kent's face and he shouts for my mother, who runs in almost immediately, as if she's been anticipating disaster. I feel like someone has lit a match at my feet and the fire is moving up, up.

"It's stridor breath," I tell my mom, the rattling sound made by a person who is dying, that moment when the breathing pattern noticeably changes—the body's unmistakable signal that the end is near. "She's dying, this is it." I can feel my whole body rise up to this obvious threat. "Mom, can't you hear that?"

"She's okay," my mom says in her best "nurse" voice (calm, efficient, a bulwark against patient alarm) and examines Charlie closely. "Now. It looks like she just has a booger. That's why her breath sounds strange. I see a little boog in there."

I am moaning and rocking from side to side. I am sure it is happening again. My baby is going to die. I know it. "It's stridor breath, it's stridor," I repeat. My bladder is about to give way. "Mom!"

"Stop it," my mother barks, and shakes her head at Kent, whose face has fallen into his chest with fear and confusion. "Mary?" he asks.

"She's not," my mom says, and then to me, in a voice that means "SNAP OUT OF IT," she says, "SHE IS NOT DYING. She just has a big booger in her little nose."

"No no no no no," I repeat.

"Emily, leave the room," my mom instructs. She's holding Charlie's head gently in one palm, and trying to maneuver the pinkie finger of her other hand into the ridiculously small baby nostril.

I shake my head and refuse to leave. My mom gives Kent a look that says *Move*, and he grabs both my arms and maneuvers me into the hallway. "It's going to be okay," he says, and shakes me gently. "The baby needs you to be calm," he warns in a terrified voice. He returns to the bedroom, and I hear my mom say, "Close the door."

"Okay," I say to the wall. "I'll stay here." I stare at a photo of Nancy and Libby on their wedding day at Chelsea Piers in New York City. I'm pregnant and wearing a striped dress— I look like a happy, round-bellied zebra wearing too much sparkly eye shadow. The newlyweds are laughing, mouths open, and we're dancing the conga or the love train or some other group dance dictated by the DJ on the dance floor just in front of glass windows that look out across the water. The lights of the city flicker and blur across the dark, still surface of the river. Surely I cannot hear devastating news while lost in a photograph depicting such great happiness of such good people. Surely. As soon as I have this thought I remember a pastor from my brief, misspent Evangelical youth warning me that "God doesn't like pride and He will get you." Bad theology, obviously, some silly quasi-Christian physics of "What goes up, must come down," but in this moment it rings true. Maybe I haven't been gotten badly enough, although it certainly seems so. Maybe there is much more to endure.

I am lit from the inside, the fire spreading, with an emotion I cannot accurately pinpoint. Existential panic? Hysteria, that loaded word used almost exclusively to describe the emotional reactions of women? *Regroup*, I tell myself, and imagine a huddle on a basketball court, a coach shouting directions, calling out plays. *Think of something. Find a way.* I land on this: a grief therapist I saw for only one session when Ronan was alive offered an instruction: to focus on colors when I was feeling anxious or sad, as if attaching a visual— a "shade," as she called it—to an out-of-control feeling might help pin it down, lessen its power. Like a Pinterest board of color-coded emotions. "When you're angry or panicked can you imagine the color red? Can you let yourself feel it and then transition to a cooler, calming color? A light and peaceful blue, a calming white? Could you make a painting?" I can make no feeling paintings in this moment and never really could. When I thought about how to conquer anxiety, the only color that came to mind was black, all of the colors blended together, like the dark mess of a child's mixed paints. "Black is the absence of color," the therapist said. This was exactly my point, and apparently my problem.

I hear my mom shout, "Got it!" and then Kent says, "Thank God," and without being summoned I burst back into the room. Charlie, having slept through this entire ordeal, is breathing in and out of both sides of her tiny nose with ease, almost soundlessly. Her new, sticky fingers are spread like little stars across her pink blanket covered in dancing monkeys. My mom holds out a pair of tweezers with a booger the size of the head of a pin balanced on the end. Kent has his hand on Charlie's head, completely covering her cap of red fuzz. "It was a booger," he says, his voice growing softer as he speaks, like a balloon slowing losing air.

"You're not supposed to use these," my mom says, meaning the tweezers, "but you"—she points the sharp tips at me—"were totally losing it." Her voice is sharp and high, tinged with elation, the feeling that comes just after panic recedes.

I, too, feel the adrenaline rush of relief (so similar to panic!), and we all laugh and cry and lightly touch the soft sleeping baby head. Kent kisses me, but I can feel the sweat on his back and his tense muscles. He was scared, too. I remind myself that he has also watched a baby die not so long ago. Ronan was not his child, but he loved him, and to see someone—anyone—die is to bear a profound witness to what awaits us all, what awaits everyone we've ever loved. To see a human body that houses someone cross that liminal space between life and death in just a breath, even after a long labor, rewrites the world, with all its pitfalls and possibilities.

We relief-laugh some more, which sounds more like heaving than laughter, and will refer to what happened this night as the "great booger incident," the first of many family stories that we will no doubt repeat to Charlie when she asks about her earliest days. After my mother goes back to bed and Kent retreats to the deck for a shot of mescal, I position my arm along Charlie's back the way I used to position my arm when Ronan was alive and slept next to me. I trace her spine with my forearm as I once traced his, sometimes for hours, working to memorize a sensation that returns now without effort. I try to root myself into the bed, which feels like it's spinning. *How am I going to do this? How am I going to live like this or parent with all this fear?* I fall asleep, but wake up in the morning with my heart pounding, as if I've slept alongside its panicked and erratic rhythm.

CHAPTER SEVEN

Ghost World

If you respect the dead
and recall where they died
by this time tomorrow
there will be nowhere to walk.

KATIE FORD, "EARTH"

When Charlie is still a newborn, each morning as we walk through the swinging doors of our bedroom into the sanctuary's main space, her gaze moves immediately to the corner nearest the now unused wood-burning stove. She smiles and coos as if she's recognizing something, or someone.

"What do you see?" I ask her. The same corner, every morning. How can this be an accident or a coincidence?

"Grrr goo goo," she gurgles, and then shrieks happily.

I ask Kent, "Do you really think the church is haunted?"

Kent's mother, Ginny, claimed to see the ghost, a fact she dropped as casually as one might the time or a compliment at a dinner party; when Kent pressed her for more details she would only tell him that the ghost was a friendly girl, probably a teenager, whom she'd seen several times during the morning.

"I think the baby sees a ghost," I tell Kent. "Maybe *the* ghost?" Charlie lunges at her father's face.

"Maybe," he says. "Maybe this ghost is excited to have another person around."

"Or central heat," I offer. "In which case we might see a lot more of her or him or it or however you refer to a ghostly person or form." The night we returned to the church after the great booger incident, the man we'd hired to build a heater took us down to the basement, showed us a network of mismatched metal tubes and what appeared to be tinfoil connectors, all of which appeared to fit with some extraordinary shape logic of his own design. He flipped the switch and held his breath. A whooshing sound like a ship's rudders beginning to turn filled the pipes, which shook as if breath had been pushed into them. It felt like being in the belly of a ship: the Super DIY Moby Dick Heating System. "I can't believe it works!" he said, practically delirious with surprise and obvious relief.

Charlie and I begin greeting the possibly real, possibly imagined ghost each morning. "Hello, ghost!" I say, and then sometimes "Holy Ghost!" just to fit with the "this used to be a functioning church" theme. Charlie looks to the corner and flashes a toothless grin. I am deliriously happy on these mornings in a way that is as close to contentment as I've ever been. I know it's the new-mother bliss feeling: everything the kid does seems like magic. This line from a Jack Gilbert poem, "A Brief for the Defense," keeps tunneling into my thoughts: "We must have the stubbornness to accept our gladness in the ruthless furnace of this world."

The ruthless furnace of those crucible years; a fire at the back, always. When Ronan was still living I sat at the boarding gate at the Denver airport and watched a dark-haired girl who was the same age as my son—who didn't and couldn't and would never move—bring a water bottle up to her lips and drink, over and over again. No trouble with the hands; the arms moved effortlessly. She had no trouble swallowing. No trouble holding up her head. No trouble at all, it seemed. I couldn't stop staring at her—her easy ability to accomplish these everyday movements appeared miraculous to me; for any child dying of Tay-Sachs, or any parent watching their child die, it was just that. Now, here is Charlie doing all of the things in the correct order, at the right times, and in the right ways, and I hope I can remember these mornings and the feeling that accompanies them: the joy, magnified by an experience of the opposite.

A few months after Kent bought the church, in 1996, he said he grew worried about ghosts and "old energy."

"What do you mean? You sound like someone who's lived in Santa Fe too long and senses spirits in every corner and tells everyone about their power animal. Energy how?"

"I found some weird shit in the basement," he continued. "I think it might have been sex stuff," he said, but then wouldn't elaborate. "My power animal is a badger, by the way."

"Of course it is! Mine's a gorilla."

"Well, there you go. We fit right in."

This was New Mexico, where a self-described shaman

might claim the ability to communicate with your ailing pet or clear your aura while also identifying your angel guides, all in one session and for a set (high!) fee. Not a surprise, then, that it was easy enough to hire an exorcist "to clear the place of whatever," Kent explained. For a hundred bucks (in cash, of course) a man who looked like Jackie Gleason moved through the sanctuary shouting, "C'mon, demon. Get out! Get on out, demon! You'd better MOVE. ON. OUT."

"Did it work?" I asked.

Kent shrugged. "I felt better. So yeah, I guess."

Despite my skepticism about spirit communication, I wonder if it's not just the ghost of the young girl Charlie sees, or some other turn-of-the-twentieth-century-era ghost, but Ronan's ghost. It doesn't seem like the strangest idea. After all, we held his memorial here on the first day of March, a cold but sunny day, with a choir in the loft singing songs composed for him and using the one sound he ever made—*GEE;* my oldest friend sang "Yellow" by Coldplay on his acoustic guitar; people offered tributes and ate cheesecake and prunes, Ronan's favorite foods. People brought their kids; one of my friends arrived pregnant, with a son she would later name after Ronan. My best friend, Emily, flew over from England yet again, the third time she'd visited New Mexico in as many years. People arrived from Los Angeles, Austin, Wyoming, and Boston. So if Ronan were to be summoned anywhere, wouldn't it be in the sanctuary, this place where both children are present, either in the flesh or in the imagination? Prior to his death, Ronan spent many hours at the church: lying on Kent's chest while we watched football; sleeping in the travel crib next to the bed. He spent his last

Thanksgiving at the sanctuary's main table, when at some point I looked at my dad holding Ronan and thought how small they both looked, Ronan's body so thin and angular, and my father's body diminished, too, by a sadness that he usually hid from me and that after Ronan's death never truly left him.

We are always living on the top of old lives, living with ghosts, real or imagined, no matter which spaces we inhabit or what kinds of lives we're living within them. This is true even if we don't believe in the afterlife (it is also scientifically and empirically true, as this is the essence of dark matter). We are always walking where others have already walked, lived, been born and died.

How can we envision or conceptualize all the old stories we live with, in, through, and alongside? In Jerusalem's Old City, it is possible to walk along the sidewalk, look down, and see the ruins and remnants of an even older Roman city, which once teemed with people and industry, drama and passion, spirit and life. All of it is gone now, literally crumbled to dust from which a few bent and precarious-looking pillars rise. Every day people walk along the city sidewalk above the older city, holding cups of coffee and bottles of water, talking on the phone, heading to work, to temple, to the mosque, to church. In New Orleans, they bury their dead above the ground. The living and the dead interact on a daily basis. When I lived in rural Texas, every evening I watched the sun set over the tiny graveyard visible through my office window. These stories connect and intertwine without our thinking about it. When my brother and I were kids riding in the back of our beat-up station wagon, each time my dad passed a cemetery we'd shout, "Hold your breath!" as if the dead buried there might notice us, make space for us before we were willing to have space made. Now when I pass a cemetery, I breathe deeply, wondering what mysteries and stories are hidden there, underground, understanding that the world would not be the world as it is without what the dead had done or left unfinished—mistakes and triumphs I will never know or have any way of knowing. I find this comforting. These stories, known and unknown, bear witness to the interconnection of the living and the dead.

At first glance, the abandonment of Jerusalem's ghost world below the living world might appear to symbolize progress, or to show how remarkable the modern world has become, having "risen above" its previous primitive ways and habits and abandoning them for a superior way of life, a "better" place in the same way heaven is often described. But the concept of resilience has not always been so deeply connected to that of the triumph of communities or individuals; it has not always been associated with "casting off" the remnants of one life for a new and better one. In the Bible, the word "glory" is often used in reference to everyday, natural objects, things that are rendered fantastic by virtue of the wonder of their mere existence, by their usefulness: the brightness of heavenly bodies, the fruitfulness of a forest, the power of a horse's snort, the intricacy of design in a well-made piece of clothing. Glory in the everyday items of everyday living.

That abandoned city, that child who no longer lives, that

person who helped build your life and give it meaning who has now left your life and possibly the world: they are holding up everything you do now, in this moment, alongside all that ever was or will be. They move beneath your feet, their hearts beating across time and memory. Whether you know it or not, sense it or not, choose to acknowledge it or prefer to ignore it, you are caught up in and supported by all the lives that came before yours.

CHAPTER EIGHT

In the Balloon

Where do you carry your dead? There's no locket
for that—hinged, hanging on a chain that greens
your throat. And the dead inside you, don't you
hear them breathing? You must have a hole
they can press their gray lips to. If you open—
when you open—will we find them folded inside?
In what shape? I mean what cut shape is made
whole by opening? I mean besides the heart.

MAGGIE SMITH, FROM "HEART"

The day before Charlie's first birthday on March 8—planned as an explosion of pink and Hello Kitty–themed napkins, plates, and balloons, and the pinkest of pink cakes—I run up the mesa behind the church to the place overlooking the Ortiz Mountains where I buried a lock of Ronan's hair a year before.

For a while after Ronan died I kept the plastic bag full of his hair in the top drawer of my dresser, tucked behind jewelry boxes and favorite cards and a clay print of his two-year-old hand made by an artist friend, which I eventually gave to my friend Weber in Boston for safekeeping. It conjured the details of his hand too precisely; it made me light-headed to look at. I also wanted it safely kept or, more accurately, guarded. Now it sits surrounded by photos of my friend's daughter, Violet. It is having a good life there.

Sometimes I'd open the bag and touch the red-gold strands, saved from his single haircut, but the hair had grown brittle and strange, as all cut hair does; it bore no resemblance to the soft, slippery mess I once kissed and stroked on his round dome of a head. After I got pregnant with Charlie, I wanted a place to scatter some of those strands. Although I'd long ago stopped believing in closure, I still had hopes for a peaceful feeling—as close to healing as I was likely to get.

When I was pregnant for the second time, I was once again teaching a summer writing workshop in Taos. My friend Elizabeth, who was part of Charlie's pregnancy from the beginning, suggested we scatter Ronan's hair from a hot-air balloon drifting over the Rio Grande Gorge, that great mouth cut into the ground not far from the Colorado border that I had, only a year before, thought about leaping into. She held out a flyer of brightly colored balloons floating above the desert against the backdrop of a spectacular sunrise. "We can ask for the one with rainbows on it," she said, laughing. I agreed.

Kent, Elizabeth, and I were out at the site before sunrise, when the wind conditions are assessed for safety. The horizon was a dark red line slowly giving way to a weak yellow glow. The balloon itself was huge but floppy, spread along the dry grass, shapeless. I kept imagining the shaking, wheels-off-the-ground, high-octane speed of an airplane, but in a *basket* in the sky, free to the elements, without any protection. We climbed with four strangers, arranging ourselves in particular places in order to evenly distribute weight, like a flower arrangement of bodies. Our pilot, a bearded man wearing an out-of-season Christmas sweater, started up the fire and the air began to fill the balloon; it swelled dramatically. Slowly and gracefully we lifted off. Within minutes we were suspended above the desert landscape with spiked mountain ranges visible from all sides, chased by our own shadow, which ran parallel to the gorge in the early morning light. A tiny, inflatable dot carrying four bodies, connecting earth and sky.

In the balloon, the concept of space and time completely disappeared, which felt odd, but not entirely uncomfortable. I felt suspended, the way I had often felt as Ronan's mother, as if I were a parent on a different planet; and the way I often did now, being pregnant again and in love again and about to be married again, but carrying a complicated past with me that I had no wish to discard. I longed to compress time, this summer and last summer, look down at that girl on the bridge, that other mother, and tell her, *Look up. All is not lost. That is never the truth. You are not at the end.*

The balloon moved like a magnet across the sky; the fire blazed, the air hissed into the balloon, and then there was a drop toward the gorge, followed by a rise. Fire, swell, dip, rise, float, repeat. We were in a slow drift that was so very high but felt close to the ground, as if you could reach out and pick up the rocks from the dry riverbeds, or pluck a bright flower from a bush. A compressed, miniature world that was also vast and unknowable.

As the balloon followed the trail of the dry riverbed on our way up and out of the gorge, we let go the wisps of Ronan's hair I'd divided into three sections. I threw mine all at once, as if I might lose my nerve—could I let go of this remnant of my son? Kent and Elizabeth let the stiff strands slip through their fingers. I felt my throat go tight, but that was it. No weeping, no sobbing, no great feeling of release. No closure, either, but the power of the moment felt meaning- ful, the kind that stamps your mind with a clearly fashioned memory—one with edges and nuance and light.

As we watched Ronan's hair tumble through the air, I wondered if the strands would be picked up by birds nesting along the gorge walls, or pilfered by a beaver to add a touch of decoration to an otherwise plain and practical structure. These creatures would interact with my son's hair as utility— for warmth, as a means to an end—and they would choose it instinctively, without thought or emotion. The natural order of the world meant that creatures living in it would carry away this hair and make use of it, and that felt hopeful.

This was, in fact, the opposite of closure: an acknowledg- ment of the openings continually offered by the world. Just as you try to pin down meaning, it scatters. Just as genes mi- grate across bone and blood and time, this hair would fall and land in places that could not be anticipated, where it would be part of a new story, one I would never know but might still imagine. Genes, bodies, moments, and meaning—all eventually scatter and are reabsorbed. This is the world prac- ticing resilience. Nothing is overcome; but also, nothing is entirely lost.

. . .

On the sunny March day of Charlie's first birthday party a year later, when I run up the mesa behind our house in Madrid where I have buried a lock of Ronan's hair, snow is still frozen in small patches along the roads, but the world is edging toward springtime. Pollen floats through the air; dust spirals up quickly from the road beneath my feet; the sky is so blue it's like the idea of blue, or the original color against which all variations are compared. The trail winds past an old hippie cemetery that I've passed many times before. Today I decide to stop and take a look. Caring for Charlie, who is active and healthy, is tiring and constant in a way that caring for a sick but immobile child was not, and I'm no longer driven by rage. I have, I think, set the anger down and, with it, my speed. I'm a slower runner, but a much happier person. Today I'm tired and need a rest.

I walk through the cemetery "gate," which is just an opening cut out of a simple wooden fence that has been mended in places by twists of black wire. Prayer flags lodged into the spokes of wooden wagon wheels serve as grave markers; a string of tattered Tibetan prayer flags is half submerged in the ground, covered in dried mud. The grave of a man who served in Vietnam and died in 1981 at the age of thirty-two is marked by a rust circle, the word SUNSHINE carved into the metal. The birth and death dates of Artensio are unknown, his grave a pointed stone with the name carved with obvious effort and at a slant, the way lovers might mark trees with their names and dates. EB LOVES KB. Don Brown's grave is marked by a silver bicycle with a wooden plaque balanced on the handles.

Nothing in the cemetery is symmetrical or well kept, and nothing is distinctly or elaborately marked; in fact, everything blends into the beige dirt. Empty bottles of vodka and gin are sunk into the ground like impromptu markers or, more likely, discarded trash from a party. Not being sure which, I leave them there. There are no towering columns, no fancy plaques. It feels more like a pit stop, or the place you end up when you take a wrong turn; but it's also a landmark on the way down the hill, letting you know that you're headed in the right direction, toward town and people and home. I stand for a moment and let the wind lift the sun-soaked dust onto my sweating arms and face. I feel a sudden peace surrounded by the stories of these people now dead on the top of a mesa in the springtime on the day of my daughter's first birthday. My daughter who lived, who is alive. And then I feel the old rage rising in me, an echo of the end of my marriage to Ronan's father.

There's a reason I tossed Ronan's hair from the basket of a sky-high balloon and why I occasionally visit this particular rock at the top of this windswept hill. I'll never know where my son's ashes are buried, or where they were scattered, or even if they were.

A week after I held Ronan's memorial in the church that was now my home, his father wrote me an email. We had planned to have a small memorial that was just family, no friends except the very closest, but I wanted something bigger: I wanted songs and food; I wanted to acknowledge all the people from so many stages of my life who had offered their support during my most difficult years. I didn't invite Ronan's father, and I didn't tell him what I was doing. Now, of course,

I understand how this must have landed on him. At the time I thought, *Why on earth would he want to come?* We had exchanged no kind words for months, even as we stood over our son's body. "He'll be mad if you don't invite him," Kent warned. "I can't imagine he would want to see any of those people again," I countered. The truth was: I didn't want him there. And Kent was right.

"You fucking cunt," Ronan's father wrote. He told me that my heart was deformed just as my body was, my spirit black. He knew me well enough to know just the right language to use, all the worst insults to volley. He offered this final wish: "I hope you have a baby and your baby DIES." He had collected Ronan's ashes, he informed me, and had scattered them in a place he swore never to reveal. "YOU WILL DIE NOT KNOWING," he promised. He sent this email not only to me but to one hundred people in my email contacts, including event managers at the bookstores where I was scheduled to read from the book I had written about our son, whom he believed I regarded as "my meal ticket." A few hours after I received his email, I began to delete email after email from strangers in Nigeria and Kiev, writing things like "You want to be my good Christian friend and even yes my lover!" "Please send bank routing number and praises to God!" Perhaps he hacked my account, I'll never know, but I had clearly misjudged my actions, and him. I stood in the kitchen of my friend's apartment in New York City, blinking out the window at the distant lights of the Empire State Building blurred by the snow falling in thick sheets. And then I went to the bathroom and threw up.

The calls from my friends and colleagues started flowing

in, the cell phone beeping and buzzing as in a crisis, as if someone had just died, but Ronan was already dead. People were sickened. I felt bewildered and stupid. "It's certainly clear why you're divorcing him," one friend wrote. I thought of a line from Jane Kenyon's translation of Anna Akhmatova's poem "A Memory of Sun": "Maybe it's a good thing I'm not your wife." I worried that Ronan's father might kill himself; it was so unlike him, the missive so outrageous and extreme. I begged one of Ronan's therapists to check on him; she called to report that he was still alive but also admitted she'd been tempted to punch him. I trembled with a fear that couldn't be identified, perhaps the fear of the wrongly accused, although of course now I understand why he would feel that I wronged him. I hated him for not wanting another baby after Ronan's diagnosis, and I punished him in every way I knew how: fury, the silent treatment, shouting and outbursts and demands. I don't regret a single minute of falling in love with Kent while Ronan was still living. My marriage to Ronan's father fractured almost immediately after our son's diagnosis, and during the last year of our son's life we did not communicate about anything but the facts: who was taking Ronan when and for what length of time. That was a mistake, and one, years later, I regret.

For days I was afraid to leave the apartment where Kent and I were staying, the rooftops and buildings along Fifth Avenue submerged in the fierce, out-of-season blizzard. I felt hunted. If I walked the streets of this city, I worried Ronan's father would somehow find me and kill me. Or maybe we would kill each other with our bare hands, fueled by our rage and disappointment and loss of love and the forever disappearance of our child.

"Is he right?" I asked everyone. "Do I deserve this?" "Is any of this true?" Everyone said no, and I did my best to believe them.

New research about people suffering from post-traumatic stress disorder suggests that, in fact, there is no "recovery" from trauma and loss—there exists no phoenix gloriously rising from the ashes as an aspirational model. Instead, the integration of an event happens incrementally, through the repeatedly walked labyrinth of time and memory, that great nexus of healing sparked by motion. It's almost as if we must metabolize the event in our bodies, as if we could eat an experience, swallow it whole, feel it churn in our bellies and bowels. I liked this idea that everything that was part of an experience becomes a part of one's physical self, part of blood and bone and water.

So it makes sense to have these thoughts about Ronan's father and Ronan on the day of Charlie's birthday; memory, after all, is a democracy, not a meritocracy. What we want to remember may not always be the image or moment that rises to the top. Embodied memory acts like an echo chamber in which all of our experiences are linked—through genetics and inheritance, yes, but also through sound, touch, and smell. We hold all the lives we've lived in this body.

At this moment, overlapping the rage and sadness that thinking of Ronan's father evokes, I remember the locket Kent gave me as a Christmas present during our first year together, when Ronan was still alive, and when I still thought

Ronan's father and I might part as friends; that we'd be able, over the years, to remember our son together, as a person who was a part of each of us. But it's true that although I miss Ronan every day, I do not miss his father. You only miss what (or whom) you continue to love.

The heart-shaped locket Kent gave me had once been a gift to his mother. Stamped into the gold was a delicate, leafy pattern and a New Mexico chile. Pressed inside was a thin strip of paper the size of a fortune from a cookie that read, "I love you, Emily." It is pressed against a matching strip of paper, written twenty years earlier, that reads, "I love you, Mom." The old and the new, intermingled and worn around the neck like a secret sign. A milagro near the heart to protect the heart; a bulwark against cruelty, a tiny but impenetrable shield.

I've heard from friends of friends that Ronan's father has moved to a new city and is taking anger management classes. "You'll never see me again," he promised in his email, and I don't want to. I wish him neither happiness nor ill, and this neutrality feels correct, perhaps even reaching toward compassion. I understand that I will never know what happened to Ronan's ashes, to that body I made inside my body. "Remember," a childhood friend wrote to me, "Ronan is in your heart forever, and you can visit him anytime you like."

Standing in this scrappy cemetery with its funky, irreverent graves and the occasional beer can resting against a stone as if someone has just christened it but neglected to pack their trash out of this rural-ish wilderness, I feel the edge of forgiveness for all that we do to each other, all the ways in which we kill love before it kills us. Maybe happiness—

complicated, showing signs of our struggle——can be revealed and appreciated only when we are stubborn enough to search for and find it, even inside sadness, perhaps especially there.

After Charlie's party, when all the other guests have gone and the sky is growing dark, Cynthia, Ronan's hospice nurse, arrives. She's later than she expected by hours. Although I don't ask, I know it's likely that she's come off a long shift helping other sick children die, other parents grieve. Yet here she is, in the deepening darkness, knocking at the door. For a time I thought I'd never want to see her again, even though she'd been so faithful, so good, so present and kind, so smart and strategic. Hospice workers, I'm told, are used to this. Why would you want to see the person who reminds you of the most difficult moment of your life? And it wasn't just Cynthia I avoided; I saw Ronan's physical therapist at the farmers' market just after Charlie was born and ducked away before she could see me, this woman who had been so patient and loving with my son. I was eating a bagel with Charlie in the front pack at a café when I saw another of Ronan's kind and generous therapists. The bread felt like chalk in my mouth; she hadn't known I was pregnant or now had a child, and I should have told her, should have shared the joy as well as the pain, but she didn't mention it, instead playing peeka-boo with Charlie and delighting in her laugh. These gracious people; why had I abandoned them when I promised myself I'd be different from the other grieving moms and keep them in the loop? The same was true with Cynthia, whom I hadn't spoken with since Ronan's death, although for the last two weeks of Ronan's life she called me every day, asking "How is today?" and then in the final days, every hour, and then every few minutes, "How is it right now?" I invited her at the last moment, and primarily out of guilt.

But when I see her standing on the porch wearing her signature bright, flowing skirt and blinking her long eyelashes in the cold, I can hardly hold back tears. I realize that, as a carrier of both tremendous hope and the most terrifying sorrow (perhaps an alternative definition of DNA itself—you get a bit of "good"; you get a bit of "bad"), she is the person I've been waiting to see all day. I can't get to her quickly enough.

Together we sit down in the main room. Charlie grips the wooden coffee table with both hands to keep her balance. As she begins to work her way around, Cynthia takes one of her hands in her own, and says, "Good job." Charlie turns her head, smiles, and says to Cynthia and me: "*GEE!*" Her voice echoes in the church's main room.

"Oh," Cynthia says, and her voice catches. "Ronan's word." She reaches for my hand. I take hers and hold it tight.

I don't know how to thank her. I can't say a word. What I want to do is something that for years I thought I'd never long to do again: I want to write a love letter to the world. "If I don't know how to be thankful enough/The rose/The gardenful/The evening light/It's nine o'clock and I can still see everything" (Wendy Cope, "If I Don't Know").

Less than two years later, I will be fully embedded in a different home, in a different life, and my friend Margaret will text me late one night, describing the weekend day at home with her three kids, how they were so good, and spent the afternoon performing shows and scenes from the *Nut-cracker* while she took down the Christmas tree. "And then they discovered balloons," she wrote, a line of words that will lead me straight back to the moment over the Rio Grande, and then to the mesa, and then to the room where a child walked in a space another child once inhabited, and so many before that.

"I'm grateful," I sputter awkwardly to Cynthia. And for a moment it's as if we are resting beneath a balloon of sky, and lifting like it.

CHAPTER NINE

Speak, Mnemosyne

Don't say it's the beautiful
I praise. I praise the human,
gutted and rising.

KATIE FORD, FROM "SONG AFTER SADNESS"

At the butterfly exhibit, inside a humid room of domed glass, diaphanous butterflies cross one another in patterns of flight so precise they seem choreographed. These bear almost no resemblance to the more ordinary butterflies you might find flitting through the yard on a sunny morning. They are truly magnificent: delicate-looking, but with impressive wingspans allowing them to fly with the strength and muscle of hummingbirds; they are nearly the size of moths, their insect cousins. Their loops and dives are practically audible, like velvet ribbons snapping the air. Charlie is two years old, and we have just moved from New Mexico to Palm Springs, where Kent has been hired as a magazine editor, and I am teaching.

As Charlie stops to investigate a flower, a red-gold wing of hair falls over her eyes and a butterfly lands on the top of her head. With obvious delight and wonder she registers the sudden, trembling weight—a fat, opulent monarch with wings so saturated in color it's as if they're wet with fresh paint. Her chubby toddler knees quiver slightly with the effort to remain still. The butterfly settles itself, opening and closing its black-and-gold wings—slowly, gently—before flying away, all without disturbing a single strand of my girl's fine hair. She straightens up to watch its flight, and then looks over her shoulder—to be sure I'm there, or maybe to see if I've seen what she's seen. "I saw," I say. "I see you."

Charlie rejoins the rush-stall staccato of the other toddlers and school-age children running along the paved and winding path lined with pink and orange flowers swaying slightly in the climate-controlled air. As she stops to observe a dazzling yellow butterfly on the thin edge of a little girl's ear, another monarch (perhaps the same one?) lands in her palm—a sleek comma of a body. The high desert light filters through the wings, brightening them until they appear almost weightless, as if they might suddenly dissolve. As if disappearing into the world might be a way of anchoring to it, precisely and completely. "Ooh," Charlie coos.

The butterfly's skinny antennae vibrate like plucked harp strings, a single note of a secret song. Charlie remains still, the butterfly balanced on her open palm. Although she is strong enough to crush this fluttering creature in her little fist, she does not. After a few moments the insect lifts off and Charlie raises her flushed face, eyes wide in the muted light, following the butterfly's airborne route until it disappears behind a tree. *What a day!* I think. *What a girl!*

I rub my damp palms on my jeans and feel ruthlessly happy. I remember standing on the edge of that high bridge in New Mexico. Some may assume that mother is gone, replaced, but I know this is not the case. She is here, in this room, with me. Ronan is gone *and* Charlie is here, spiriting through this lit space like the sprite in a kid's favorite storybook, sure-footed and strong and able, practically breathless with glee. I think of a line from Jack Gilbert's poem "A Brief for the Defense": "We must risk delight." Against all odds, against all past and future sorrows, yes. But this risk can feel unsettling to take, like staking a claim. A wall of anger acts as it is intended to: as a defense against risk, a defense against feeling. And it's feeling that warps us, changes us, forges us, challenges us. It is far more difficult to give in to the softening than to stay behind a wall.

On this day in the butterfly room, I watch the toddlers winding through the warm and colorful space, totally absorbed in the light, the feelings, the sights and sounds, fully present as they casually grab one another's hands in passing and then just as easily untangle fingers in order to chase another insect zipping through the fragrant air. The butterflies embody delicacy and strength, lightness and power, endurance and release: all these elements held in a seemingly effortless balance.

What I see in these insects is a resilience released from the heroic images with which it is often paired, the implication being that focused effort and striving might lead to wholeness or happiness. This is a powerful revelation. All creatures are built to make efforts to survive, but this is different from intentional striving. To fight for life is what makes us alive; to want to live to the final possible moment, to the outer reaches of our abilities, is what makes us human.

In Nabokov's *Speak, Memory*, he describes the dead as "dear, bright selves." Is this why he loved butterflies so much, referring to himself as "godfather to an insect"? "Literature and butterflies are the two sweetest passions known to man," he wrote, and given his arduous work to discover new species, one is inclined to believe such an earnest declaration. Perhaps he saw butterflies as visitations of the dead. The living walk among the dead. The dead move with us who still live, reminding us where we've been, and also where we're headed.

Nabokov knew what it meant to lose everything and begin again: born into great wealth and privilege, his father lost everything in 1917 after involvement in a movement to establish democracy in Russia. Five years later his father was shot to death in Berlin by a monarchist. Nabokov lived the rest of his life as a professor, but he remained a passionate student of lepidopterology, scurrying around in sensible walking shoes, net in hand, "on the hunt," as he called it. A butterfly, captured and now spread "wide open on its pin (though fast asleep)." Dead, yes, but also: safe from the ravages of time.

As I am leaving the butterfly exhibit holding a sweating and glassy-eyed Charlie, who is limp with fatigue, long strands of damp hair curling around her ears, I ask the docent responsible for ushering people in and out at carefully paced intervals: "Do the butterflies die if they break free of this room?" The thought is both sickening and oddly appealing. Maybe they feel confused in there. Maybe it would make more sense to roam above the Mexican wolves and the cheetahs and the leopards, the giraffes and African hedgehogs and gazelles in the Living Desert. How would they survive under normal (read: brutal) life conditions, particularly given their brief life spans, ranging from three days to a year? Would they be killed as quickly as I squash the centipedes and tiny spiders I sometimes spot scurrying across my living room floor? Would a scientist wielding a net trap them with a flick of a wrist? (Apparently Nabokov had a signature wrist movement for this; he was very skilled at trapping insects.)

"Butter-fwhy!" Charlie cries. Later I will learn that Nabokov, after once hearing a child say "flutter-by," thought a revision of the word "butterfly" might be "better fly," that is, "one bigger and brighter than other flies."

The docent shakes his head. "A butterfly with an injured wing can still fly," he tells me, "it just won't look the same." He pauses. "I mean, they just go. Get on with it." This resonates with me: the idea that a rupture—in the body, heart, or mind—that isn't fully mended doesn't prohibit life or the full living of it, through both joy and pain. In the case of butterflies, this might be a permanent, prominent defect that affects—but doesn't entirely eliminate—flight. Butterflies don't think about being uneven or inelegant or made incorrectly or recently damaged as they move, but instead carry on with what they were designed to do: fly. Live. Watching a splinted butterfly stumble up into the air or an injured bird struggle with a broken wing is uncomfortable for humans. Yet the lack of self-consciousness in the awkwardness or even "incorrectness" of that movement is, for me, the epitome of resilience. It's less about finding a hidden source of strength and more about softening to the unfairness and beauty of the world, accepting its smooth grace as well as its sharper edges. Pain with benefits. Happiness with blood in it.

"Thanks," I tell the docent again. He looks bewildered. "Thanks so much," I say a few more times until I realize I've been shaking his hand all this time and let go.

Although it's February in the Coachella Valley, carrying Charlie on my hip I break a sweat almost immediately as I walk back to the parking lot. It's high season in the Palm Springs area, and tourists of every age, shape, and size are roaming the paths, wearing visors and sensible shoes, looking at the animals, and queuing up to offer food to the giraffes at their hourly feedings. A man using a walker; a little girl with prescription-grade glasses secured to her head with a wide elastic band; a woman in a motorized wheelchair; and me, the mother with the limp who lost a child—one loss seen, the other unseen. All of us embodied, all imperfect, all on the move. Alive.

No wonder the elegant imbalance of butterflies, and humans, appeals to me. As Nabokov noted, "All butterflies are beautiful and ugly at the same time—like human beings." And just as he loved lepidopterology, and linked it intimately with his love for and writing of literature, he also thought of butterflies as an obsession, a mania, a sickness. Two things at once, two feelings at once, two realities at once, like those train tracks from my high school years, two straight lines in a field. The living of two lives at once, literally and metaphorically. Exactly.

When I was in high school, my dad dragged me to a fundraising dinner for the Raptor Education Foundation, a nonprofit dedicated to protecting injured birds—owls and hawks and especially eagles, these last birds being those that are most often the victims of deliberate attacks. The more regal and beautiful the bird, it seems, the more people long to destroy it.

That night, a bald eagle with a wing that had been partially shot off by a hunter was perched on his rescuer's arm, the arduous and painful-sounding process to recovery explained in graphic detail, the bird blinking into the buzzing lights of the church basement where the dinner was held. There were several other injured birds making the rounds as attendees chewed on lukewarm roast beef and lumpy mashed potatoes, the rescuers hoping to elicit enough sympathy to encourage people to open their checkbooks and contribute to the cause.

These asymmetrical birds and their awkward, ungraceful flight, their spastic flutter of broken wings, reminded me of my own body. As a result of a birth defect, my left foot was amputated when I was four, and I'd worn a wooden leg ever since—until 1992, a very primitive one. The lurching movements of those birds mirrored my own hitch-and-drag gait, and I was relieved when the evening finally ended. I'd seen bald eagles on hikes through the Rocky Mountains, soaring through pine-scented air crackling with sunshine. I didn't like to see them in this state, in this way: damaged. Later I would learn that the bones of birds are hollow to allow for easier flight, and I would remember these birds and how weighted by sadness they appeared, not light or buoyant at all.

As we were driving home to the Denver suburbs that were, in the early 1990s, at the beginning stages of endless sprawl with an identical strip mall on every other corner, the stars were lined up, crisp and orderly, along the dark dome of the sky. Both the Big and Little Dippers were easy to identify, the ropes of light snapped into familiar geometric shapes. Long dead, those stars were still scattering light, made of some material that created this impressive celestial symmetry when so many living things on the earth had to walk around wounded and damaged. The thought gave me a restless, lonely feeling, a nugget of discomfort in my belly. Those stars were lucky, I thought, in ways that birds or people could never be. I wondered if it would have been better for the birds if nobody had saved them, if they'd simply been allowed to die. How much pain could one animal withstand? How much crap did a person really want to live with, or through? What bird wanted to live under a roof for the rest of its life? Was it worth being an eagle if it meant being paraded around banquet tables while people nodded at you with pity, all paths to real flight now rendered impossible? "What else can left-behind birds offer but their own shapes cut from the paper dark?" (Maggie Smith, "Mountain Child"). Was it enough? At the time I didn't think so, but later I would believe otherwise.

In some versions of the myth of the phoenix, the bird dies

in a conflagration of fire and beak, bone, and wing, the death of its predecessor the precondition for its new life; in others, it simply decomposes before it is reborn. In this latter iteration it's unclear how much of the original animal is retained, or if the bird that rises from this pile of flesh is a wholly new creation. But in all versions, it is as if the miracle and the curse are held together, an intimate pairing, terrible but beautiful.

After we leave the butterfly room, and are driving along Highway 111 back to our rental house in Cathedral City with Charlie snoozing in her car seat, a few crushed Goldfish crackers stuck to her sweaty palm, the phoenix appears to me less like its triumphant mythical depictions, and more like those injured birds that I watched being paraded around a church basement while people picked at their Jell-O desserts and pitied them. What if, instead of heroically bursting from the fire, a weakened and traumatized bird rises awkwardly, just barely, careening through a wall of sky on fire, entirely uncertain of what fate awaits when it finally clears the smoke? Why can't this mess be a triumph? Why can't basic survival be a kind of glory? Why do we envision a pristine and painless resurrection—when the world shows us, time and time again, how messy these processes really are? Charlie loves the classic children's book *The Very Hungry Caterpillar*, but the story makes the journey of transformation seem cute, easy, and certainly bloodless. The little green caterpillar chews through the shiny, delicious apple, pickle, pie, cake, sausage, muffin, and finally eats through a final leaf (a palate cleanser); then, on the next page, he appears as a butterfly, spread across the final two pages in a beautiful, colorful, fully transformed state. But transformation requires work, even if it's not always the kind you can think your way through.

Nabokov observed that butterfly larvae "undergo a complete metamorphosis from caterpillar to pupa, or chrysalis, to adult, one of the most astonishing transformations in the biological world. From caterpillar to pupa is a specialized molt, which all animals with exoskeletons must do in order to grow. But it's the emergence of the butterfly itself from the pupa that is so remarkable, as the outline of the fully formed insect is visible through the pupa itself. The ghostly outline of the adult butterfly, the features of its head and body and the contours and lineaments of its compacted wings can be seen eerily embossed on the surface" (*Nabokov's Blues*). (He also likened the sense of a story beginning to emerge to "the pattern showing through the wing cases of the pupa.")

Plenty of creatures grow through this ability to transform, to struggle, to molt—from the water flea, no bigger than a staple, to wall lizards and the common garden snakes that shed their skin. The Mexican red-knee tarantula outgrows its exoskeleton; the Amazon milk frog sometimes makes a meal of its discarded skin; other frogs molt every few days. Insects have instead of backbones exoskeletons made of chitin, a matrix of proteins that is similar to the keratin in human hair and nails. This watertight barrier is an armor that doesn't allow for expansion; eventually, when the animal outgrows it, it must be shed. Grief might be described as a specialized molt of emotion. All of us are required, at some point, to transform in some way (mentally, physically, emotionally) in order to live. It doesn't make us brave or special or worthy of being singled out. It makes us living creatures made of malleable, mortal, and, yes, resilient, stuff.

If myths have the phoenix, historians trace the existence of butterflies, alongside dinosaurs, to the cusp of the Cretaceous (130 million to 70 million years ago) and Eocene periods (about 50 million years ago). Butterflies have been at the messy transformation game for a long time, and the earliest records of them already place them in an exalted position. The word *butterfly* is a Germanic inheritance . . . its origin is obscure. One guess is that the emergence of the insects in warm weather coincided with butter-producing time. Another is that throngs of yellow Brimstones, one of the first butterflies to appear in the European summer, reminded people of the color of butter. In folklore, butterflies, or witches in the shape of butterflies, stole milk and butter. Beautiful in flight, yes, but also: thieves.

A few days after the trip to the butterfly exhibit, I find numerous websites dedicated to "How to Care for a Butterfly with a Broken Wing: 11 Steps," and other articles under "First-Aid for Butterflies."

I continue reading and spot this: *Resilin:* linked to the word resilience in both name and definition, as the elastic substance of cross-linked protein chains found in butterfly wings, and in the wings of other insects as well. *Resilin's* Latin root is *resilire:* to leap back, to recoil; the ability of a substance or object to spring back into shape. Perhaps this accounts for the surprising fortitude of butterflies. Those paper-thin wings! Those pin-sized antenna! The word implies a rebound, a bounce, a return—active, dynamic movement. Elasticity is a key component here, as the new shape relies on the old shape to function, even if that shape has changed. The old and the new must work together. Although the textbook definition indicates that "desire to survive" is an essential characteristic of resilience, along with the ability to accommodate abnormal threats and events, the ability of a material to absorb and release energy and return to its original state, adaptability, and interdependency—it seems to me that resilience is not always a function of the *desire* to survive. Either you survive, or you don't. There's no fault, no moral judgment, assigned to either outcome.

When Charlie is nearly five, while we are staying at my parents' house in Wyoming during the Christmas holiday, we are punched out of sleep by high winter winds that rattle the glass as forcefully as a tornado might. An earthquake of wind like fists pummeling the roof, the walls, the doors. The dark shadows of the trees in the few weak streetlights bend and reach.

"Is that a ghostes?" Charlie asks, using her uniquely incorrect pronunciation of the word. Her long lashes blink in the moonlight.

"It's just wind," I tell her. The glass panes tremble inside their wooden frames. Frozen branches knock against the house. "A lot of wind."

She considers this, and then asks: "Do you remember that dead butterfly we saw once? At home? It was brown."

My kid's treasure box of a memory continually astounds me. I scroll back through my own memory file cabinet. "At home in California? The monarch?"

"Yes. Moe-narch. He was brown with yellow dots. His wing was broked." When she brought it to me near the end of summer, one of its wings was torn off, an oddly clean break, as if someone had done it intentionally.

"Yes, he couldn't fly at all, and so he died."

"We put him back into the ground?"

"Yes, we dug a little hole for him under a tree. What made you think of him?"

"Just that if he grabbed a piece of that wind he could fly again."

And with that, she falls asleep. I lie awake for an hour or so, thinking about wind carved into pieces, wind-rafts and wind-boats carrying the bodies of butterflies on a final, glorious flight. I also think about the grief counselor Kent and I have taken Charlie to visit with several times.

In the fall, Charlie had begun telling anyone who would listen—strangers at the park, her teachers and friends, random people in the grocery line—that she had a brother who died and that his name was Ronan. She reported this news matter-of-factly, without obvious emotion, but instead with a certitude that was off-putting to many of the people she chose to tell. Little is more disarming than a four-year-old telling you about the death of her brother. The most common response was Oh! Followed by a stuttered and awkward I'm sorry or I'm sorry to hear that, responses that she wasn't around to hear, having already sprinted off to the swing set or the duck pond. She didn't seem worried or upset. It was a fact, and that was that. At school she decorated a paper cutout of her hand, and written on each little finger was something she was thankful for: on the pinkie finger the teacher had written for her, For Ronan, my brother who died.

"It's probably a good thing that she treats it literally, as a fact," I said to Kent hopefully. We decided to listen to what she said about him, and never correct her or shut her down, but simply to invite her to express herself.

One night, sitting on her pink potty before bath time, Charlie asked me if she could get what Ronan had, and if she did, would she die and be dead forever, too?

I felt like someone hit a panic button in the middle of my forehead. "No," I said. "Ronan was born with a very rare disease that made his body too sick to live in the world. You can never get what he had." But as I said that in the most reassuring voice I could manage, I thought of the people I knew who had died of cancer in their twenties and thirties; I thought of the other kids, who, like Ronan, were dying and would die of infantile, juvenile, or late-onset Tay-Sachs.

"Okay," she said, sounding entirely unconvinced.

"Would you like to talk to someone about Ronan that's not Mommy or Daddy?"

"Okay," she said, and then proudly stood up to show me an enormous pile of poop. "I had a burrito," she explained. I laughed.

In the tub, she looked at me and said, "But even though Ronan is dead, we think of him and so it's like he's alive."

"Yes, that's true," I told her, and handed her a few of her rubber ducks.

"That's called memory, Mommy," she said, pointing at me as if to say, *Remember this.*

Some of my most important conversations with Charlie happen during bath time. I've explained to her why my prosthetic leg needs to come off in order for me to get into the bath with her, which led to a clever nickname: Leggy, which then became a Lego figurine she made at Legoland, complete with mismatched limbs. Bath time is when she tells me about a fight she had at school—"He got to feed the turtle and it's not fair!"—or lets me know that she actually doesn't like soccer and doesn't want to keep doing it.

During the first session with the children's grief therapist, who had a kind face and long, dark hair, Kent and I sat in the waiting room outside the closed door, flipping mindlessly through outdated copies of *Psychology Today* and listening to Charlie's chirpy, cartoonlike voice chattering away in the other room. We couldn't hear what she was saying through the door (although we later admitted we were both trying to decipher a word, a sentence, something), but as I read the same paragraph four times in an article called "The Science of Smart," I worried that she was expressing fear, or anger, or great sadness that I hadn't done enough to placate.

"There's no guidebook for this kind of parenting," I told Kent as a way of reminding myself. There was much more at stake here than how to allocate resources, carve out quality time, or find a good school; this was about finding the appropriate words to deliver this doozy of an existential fact: that without the death of a brother you would never meet or know, you would not be alive, your parents would never have met. What kid wants to carry that around? What neat organizational box could hold that conundrum? As my friend Dale's then ten-year-old son, Aaron, said to me after Charlie was born, "Ronan died, which is sad. And Charlie is here, which is happy. It's like two sides of the same thing."

"There's no real guidebook for *any* kind of parenting," Kent responded, which made me feel marginally better.

After forty-five minutes, Charlie bounced out of the therapist's office, her usual chatty and cheerful self.

"She did great," the therapist said, but offered no more information. *What does "great" mean in this context?* I wondered. "Do you want to make another appointment?" We did.

"Do you want to tell Mommy what you talked about?" I asked Charlie in the car. Kent gave me the side-eye as if to say, *It's supposed to be private.* Or, as Charlie demands when she wants to be alone: "Privacy!"

"I told her I see Ronan sometimes on the wind or in corners." *On* the wind?

"You do?" I looked at Kent, whose eyes were wide, but also still held a warning: *Don't push.* "Where, honey?"

"Can I get a Happy Meal?" she asked, and then quickly changed the topic to the rainbow unicorn she wanted for Christmas. "Can you text Santa about the Barbie Dreamhouse, too?" she asked. I texted myself and held up the phone so she could hear the ding. "Done!"

On Christmas Eve Day, before we opened presents, Charlie began building a "project" in the middle of the living room floor. She decorated a pink plastic chair with ribbons and strips of shiny wrapping paper; she asked my mom to get her a candle, which she set on a table made of my old wood blocks painted in primary colors. She recruited a few dolls and the "prettiest" of the plastic planets that had come in her solar system kit, which we planned to hang on the wall and light up in her room at home. After that was all done, she stood up and said, "For all who have died. Ronan. Ronan. For people who have died," in a singsong chant, using a low voice not unlike the one my dad used during Lenten chants. She waved her hands in the air and walked around the chair and the lit candle. Finally, she closed her eyes, bowed her head, blew out the candle, and said, "Can we open some presents now?"

This night in Wyoming as the wind continues its familiar racket, I think about the way in which kids understand liminality or "in between" states of being in a more authentic way precisely *because* they think so literally, which perhaps renders them more capable than adults at living with two realities simultaneously, or able to do it with less pain.

A few summers ago, my aunt and uncle lost their house to a tornado that leveled every house on the street where they'd lived for over forty years. All that was left was the brass pendulum from the clock that stood in their front room and that I remember well. The clock striking time when I stayed up all night playing cards with my cousins; family portraits taken in front of it and pressed into books that disappeared into a cone of wind and dust and thunder. The pendulum, encased in glass, is now mounted on the wall of their condo. All that's left of the life lived in a house that no longer exists.

There is another fierce rattle of the panes, but this time Charlie doesn't stir. I fully expect an object to fly through the air, which is not uncommon during this type of weather in the High Plains (an empty trash can that someone forgot to weight with rocks; a frozen tree branch shaken loose and airborne; a plastic chair someone neglected to rescue from the deck because it was buried in snow), but nothing happens. I fall asleep to the howl and the hum, my body a barrier between the window and Charlie.

I remember that no matter the sound—a monitor tracking oxygen levels for your lost boy, beeping and lit red every few seconds as if to warn of a burglar; or the hiss and suck of a suction machine dislodging mucus from your lost boy's lungs; your living girl's soft snore, or her restless mutterings during a dream; even the wildness of a twisting sky over your head where a roof used to be; if you listen to it long enough, you will eventually find a place of peace—a sanctuary—inside it.

CHAPTER TEN

Build This Ship to Wreck

True, we mold the world.
Something passes through our hands—
a pig, a person, clay or alloy,
some living material—and the handling
shapes the thing. . . .
But in certain rare moments, the gears kink,
sputter, and reverse. Then objects
flash us with their genius.

JENNY GEORGE, FROM "INFLUENCE"

The Hebrew word for "sanctuary" is "mikdash" (מִקְדָּשׁ),
which comes from the root word "kadash" (קָדַשׁ), "to be
set apart as sacred." A mikdash is therefore a "set apart space"
or a "holy place" that represents something treasured—
a place of beauty and worship, a refuge, a place of rest, and
sometimes that rest is permanent.

Sanctuaries exist wherever we find the sacred; in places
that hold us away from harm; in spaces where we feel love
and connection. "Sanctuary": from the Latin *sanctuarium*,
meaning set apart as a refuge from danger or hardship. I
have known so many sanctuaries. A wild hilltop cemetery

near San Francisco, grave washers at work, deer twitching their ears in the nearby woods, the ocean in the distance hidden by fog; hundreds of pairs of baby shoes lined up in the children's chapel in Chimayo, New Mexico, where colorful wooden birds hang from the ceiling and perch along the baptismal font; the dusty vestry of a Presbyterian church streaked with light, Charlie crawling along the heart-shaped train of my dress; a hospital room during a childhood Christmas, red poinsettias arranged in circles around the bed; a pub in northern England, the light low and the conversation bright; my flimsy, one-person-at-a-time balcony in Dublin, watching the summer light fade but never entirely before the sun rose again; a guest room in a terraced house in South London, looking through the window into the school yard next door, rain shattering on the roof, and a friend promising, "You're going to live through this"; a porch in Southern California, the way palm trees hold light on a steamy summer afternoon, shaking shadows across the yard. Any space with walls or without might become a sanctuary; any object might signify one; any memory might offer one up; any vessel might take you there. Our minds treat these places as things: mobile, tactile, ships set sail in the ocean of memory.

For the Vikings, a sanctuary was a place of movement, a mobile vessel symbolizing life and death. Ships ferried the Vikings to the edges of the world, expanding their sense of home and purpose; these same ships acted as burial vessels. Ships protected travelers on arduous journeys across waterways and seas, and ushered them to the afterlife, often in those same waters.

In my research about resilience I discover the word first

appeared in reference to Viking ships. The Vikings were the first to select particular types of wood to build ships for their exploratory journeys, weighing the material's abilities to adapt and recalibrate—the necessary attributes to withstand the effects of a turbulent sea crossing. Depending on their region of origin, they chose pine and oak for the wood's ability to adapt to changes in weather and water. A material that could tolerate change without being destroyed; wood that was resilient. The best, or "green," wood, recently felled and fresh, was chosen for its flexibility, and shipbuilders followed the grain to maximize strength and flexibility without adding weight. A Viking ship was clinker built, meaning the outside, or exoskeleton, was built first, and the frame then placed inside it. Overlapping planks meant that the boat wasn't held tightly together; this was intentional, to maximize the transmission of force between the hull and the tools that caused forward motion; namely, the oars and the sail. For the sails, wool was chosen for the ability to stretch and soften, making it less likely than a stiff or outwardly stronger sail to burst during a storm or squall. No Viking sails have ever been found; only the fragments of a fourteenth-century woolen sail discovered in a church sanctuary in Norway. The rigging was made of flexible, soft horsehair to minimize cuts and burns on the many hands it passed through. Wool dipped in pine resin—"resin," the same root word for the proteins in butterfly wings—wedged between the planks helped keep the boat as watertight as possible.

But it was choosing the right wood that constituted this first critical step in ancient shipbuilding. Michael Snyder, in an article written for the Vermont Forest Service, explains the unique "wound response" of wood: "wounds will always remain within, but trees compartmentalize these injured areas to prevent decay and allow new growth to continue outward." Because they "put up with all manner of injury and insult during their lives," they are uniquely suited to be fashioned into boats. It is not uncommon for a mature tree in an average forest to "have had a thousand wounds." Like a person. Like a bird. Like a life. Even cut wood is resilient, able to adapt, a.k.a. weaken, when it needs to as it is manipulated by shipbuilders.

Trees don't repair their wounds the way humans do. There are no scars that turn white and smooth after a set period of time; instead, a new layer of bark is added to the cone shape, which is why we see rings in trees.

When a cell is damaged, a tree cannot go back and fix or replace it. But it can limit the damage from any given injury by containing it . . . from the rest of the still-growing tree. The trick is in sealing, not healing. Trees close wounds in two separate processes that create both chemical and physical boundaries around the damaged cells. First, they produce what is sometimes called a reaction zone, altering the chemistry of the existing wood surrounding a wound and making it inhospitable to decay organisms. Then, they build a barrier zone to compartmentalize the injured tissue with new tissue called 'callus' or 'wound wood' growing outward. If all goes according to plan, the callus growth covers and seals the wound and allows new uncontaminated wood to grow over and beyond it. The 'ribs' of new growth separate the wood present during the injury from the new wood formed after.... Wounds remain encased and the trees simply grow around them.... Every wound ever suffered remains within a tree."

Even after a tree is felled to serve a different purpose, these wounds serve the wood's new purpose. The damage is neither wasted nor overcome. Instead, it is folded into the utility of the substance. Without the wounds, there would be less functionality. Wounded wood is more flexible under stress, improving its functionality no matter what purpose it eventually serves.

In 1994, when I lived in Dublin as an international student in Hebrew and biblical studies, there were regular news stories about the discovery of pieces of Viking ships or shards of a Viking oar that were being unearthed as a result of the country's construction boom. Locals referred to it as "the Viking frenzy." Historians and average citizens alike worried that you could never know entirely what priceless historical treasures might be in the ground in just the place where that car park or new block of flats was going up. "It's construction paper houses going up over medieval settlements. A feckin' tragedy," my neighbor lamented each morning when we left the building together: he to work, I to a 9:00 A.M. lecture.

Dublin was a crucial Viking settlement—named Dubh Linn or "black pool." The quays, a part of the city's history, were also a part of its literary history, with a notable appearance in James Joyce's short story "The Dead," which takes place on Usher's Island, directly across the river from my apartment on Usher's Quay. I held my hand over my mouth in the construction dust on my way to Trinity College as workers struggled to excavate what might turn out to be a shard of ancient ship, a container carrying settlers that founded this city so many now called home; myself, for a time, included.

Wood and water; concrete and stone. These were the materials of everyday survival for people whose ways and manner of life would be unrecognizable to us. The architects and artisans of these things were long gone, but to see them, to know them, to imagine what these things might feel like beneath our hands or carrying our bodies, connects us to the history of all the world's sacred places, and to the world itself in all of its unknowability and strangeness. Unearthing these objects makes our own existence both more complicated and more familiar. Imagination unlocks the mystery, and also preserves it.

I know a thing or two about wood, as its inherent strengths and weaknesses were a part of my earliest and most potent embodied memories. For twenty years I wore a prosthetic limb made of wood, a tough, bright pine, not dissimilar from the material out of which Viking ships were made. Shape-shifting remains a daily task of mine—leg is attached, leg is removed. Leg wears out; parts are replaced. The process of creating a leg requires molds and casts that are shaped and then reshaped to accommodate changes in the body: weight gain and loss related to adolescence, pregnancy, or any other kind of growth.

For years that wooden leg with its metal hinges and rope straps and stretchy cloth sock and bouncy foam foot was a part of my body, incorporated both into my daily movements and into my self-image and self-understanding. It was an object, yes, but it was also a part of me. I resented it, but the thought of losing it or being seen without it made me sick to my stomach with terror. A reluctant sanctuary, but a sanctuary nonetheless. The body and the leg quickly and easily separated from each other (and had to at key points during the day), but they were not separate. Sometimes this felt confusing. Until I reached puberty I didn't think about it much. As an adult, I think about it only after the initial moment of removal before shower or bath or bed, when I feel most vulnerable. What if, for some reason, I have to run?

When I was a young girl I loved the process of having a new leg made. As it was in shipbuilding, wood used for prosthetics was chosen for an ability to withstand movement and activity. I was an active kid, and that wood weathered almost everything—rain, crashes on roller skates and swing sets, the occasional fall from a tree—breaking only once, when the hollow calf was hit full force from behind with a croquet mallet wielded by my brother. Each time I grew—an inch, a quarter inch, half an inch—a new wooden circle was added to the ankle, like rings on a tree, and by the time I had fully grown out of the leg, there might be six or seven rings of various shades of brown at the ankle stacked one on top of the other.

The first step in making a leg was to fashion the cast. The prosthetist wrapped long ropes of wet plaster around my stump, working his way to the top of my hip, scooping his palm around the bottom and holding it there for a few moments for the initial setting phase. I pressed the plaster-covered stump against his hand and stood still for about fifteen minutes, holding the edge of the table, my legs slightly apart, waiting for the plaster to set so the leg could be built around this hardened base.

In the early 1990s, with the technological innovations born of helping veterans after war injuries, my legs became more technologically and aesthetically advanced, made of carbon and silicone, not wood. Yet the cast-making process remained the same. The cast came first, and each time there was a growth spurt, there was a recast, and each cast was kept, the way parents keep the first plaster art projects of their children: those lumpy dinosaurs and misshapen hearts. Leg casts were slipped off, not cut off like surgery casts.

Along the "cast wall" in the back room of my prosthetist's office in Colorado hang the casts that symbolize my adulthood—the first cast as a college student; then the cast as a graduate student; the cast before Ronan; the first pregnancy cast; the cast after Ronan's birth; the second pregnancy cast; the cast after Charlie's birth. Sockets need to be replaced when they are sweaty and worn, and the casts were kept as reusable molds in case I got pregnant again, or gained or lost weight—one of the casts was bound to match with whatever shape my body took. These casts are parts of me, but the products of a technician's hands. They are foreign objects that shift with my body, that allow my passage through the world. When the molds are mounted on the wall, they are just that—objects, things—and yet when animated by a living form, they are vessels of safety, symbols of resilience. Sanctuaries.

. . .

As a definable term, "resilience" was introduced into the English language in the seventeenth century. In its initial appearances it was used specifically to describe the fortitude of objects and materials; it did not refer to individuals or their internal journeys or stages of emotional growth. Up until the nineteenth century "resilience" continued to be a quality and a descriptive term assigned to things, and not to people or communities or economies. It was all about stuff you could touch and hold. A ship you could crawl into, running your hand along the length of the grain, feeling the evidence of its journey in the knots and bumps and cracks; a tool you could toss from palm to palm, feeling its weight, calculating its utility, then sailing away.

It is in direct reference to things that the word "resilience" made its *written* debut in 1818, discussing effective methods of shipbuilding. Scholarly work examined timber's properties in an effort to explain why some types of wood were able to accommodate sudden and severe loads without breaking, and the circumstances that led to iron eventually taking wood's place. A *modulus of resilience* was invented: a metric; a means of assessment, a way to determine not strength but resilience, which were not synonymous. It makes sense that the question how would this kind of wood survive this sea crossing from here to here? might easily move to questions about how the *self* survived physical and mental turbulence, especially as medical technology advanced and people managed to survive calamities and diseases that decades or even a few years earlier would have killed them. The word continued to evolve when philosophers and theologians fashioned ideologies and theories of morality and right action around the definition of an intact and internal metaphysical self, one that did not necessarily rely on the world but was designed to "rise above" calamities, atrocities, sorrows, and the precarious grind of everyday life when it was so easy to be thrown off course, or "leeway," in a mariner's terms.

Modern applications of the term "resilience" are used to examine organizational structure, economic shifts, and even climate change, yet the precise definition of the word remains elusive and problematic, even as it is used with increasing regularity by policy makers, politicians, psychologists, and people having a casual chat at the grocery store about a difficult time someone might be experiencing.

Discovering these connections between history and resilience in the year after Ronan's death, thinking about wood and warp and water as a new mom with a newborn whose body was barely the length of half of my arm, I felt an unexpected but unmistakable relief. *This* is why trying to hold everything together when Ronan was dying was so exhausting! *This* is why making a new life was wonderful, but also difficult—the other life bled through because they were both fully in play, happening parallel to each other, the grief and the love together. The ship of my life had been warped and rebuilt and broken and then built again; the history of its making and evolution was there in its shape.

This is why, when people told me I was resilient and understood that word as an expression of my having broken free from grief, of having overcome the trauma of a death, it didn't resonate, and in fact actually pissed me off. All that time I wanted to prove that I wasn't just a tragic sob story, that I could beat back the forces of despair, and so I walked around with a stupid smile on my face until I was alone in my office, my car, my bedroom, where I would scream and shout and sob and curse. I thought to prove that I was resilient I had to prove I was strong, make a show of powering through, but it was just that—a show, a façade, a lie. I couldn't keep and wasn't keeping anything together. I went on trying, because I felt that steeling myself and not allowing room for breakage was expected of me; to soften and to warp would be to fail, and if I was already failing to protect my child, where did that leave me? It was a vicious and harrowing cycle. I was resilient, yes; but *because* I was broken and morphing. I wish now that I had been more open about the true growing pain of that shift, even if it frightened people, even if it frightened me to be so unhinged.

When Ronan was sick, the work was giving medicine, mashing food, checking machines, changing diapers, giving baths, and long moments of silence and dread. The list was the love; the list was the work; the list was the living, the proof of life. When Charlie was a baby it was the same, although without the medicine or machines or dread. This, too, was life.

And so is this: alongside the wonder of a new child after one has died and the thrill of a (finally) happy marriage after both partners had unhappy ones, there are chores to do, bills to pay, dishes and clothes to wash and put away, all sorts of practical logistics to consider and negotiate, financial concerns.

Although all Viking ships were open to the elements and had no lower decks to act as protection from the sea during a crossing, ships were built differently for various purposes: the longship for warriors attempting the rough passage through Russian rivers and the Caspian Sea; the heavier cargo ship for merchants carrying heavy goods; and the smaller ships that never ventured beyond the home waters. These tiny ships were built for daily domestic life, shuttling people, goods, secrets and scandals and bits of news from harbor to harbor, island to island.

No matter the size and purpose of the ship, the Vikings understood that if they did not allow for weakness and breakage, there would be no passage, no journey, no progress. That's exactly how we should build our lives: prepared for openings of whatever kind. Wood gone wonky post-trauma can make a boat more functional. The mistakes and the scars make the actual material more viable, more able to withstand attacks, which is partly about allowing the warp and damage to penetrate and shift the material. When wreckage is expected or even inevitable, it hones the ability of the material or the person or the relationship to exhibit both fragility and strength. The key is opening to it. The most functional ships, lives, relationships, moments are—in fact—sometimes built to wreck, and also, sometimes, to stay, to anchor.

CHAPTER ELEVEN

The Project of Living

Things outlast us, they know more about us than we know about them: they carry the experiences they have had with us inside them and are—in fact—the book of our history opened before us.

W. G. SEBALD

The viciousness of still objects is sometimes amazing. I'm sure that the damned walls appear for the sole purpose of showing me the windows in which I saw my only sister's face, pale as a wafer, for the last time.

ELSA BINDER, WRITING IN HER DIARY FROM STANISŁAWÓW, POLAND, IN 1942, FROM *SALVAGED PAGES: YOUNG WRITERS' DIARIES OF THE HOLOCAUST*

What could be more harrowing, more of a "test" of one's resilience, than to be a child during the Holocaust? Alexandra Zapruder is the editor of *Salvaged Pages: Young Writers' Diaries of the Holocaust*. Alexandra read and edited existing and preserved journals faithfully kept by children during the Holocaust—some of the writers lived, others died. Their daily conditions included the threat of starvation; lack of medical care; physical and emotional abuse; vicious and rampant diseases in cramped, unsanitary conditions; and terrifying, constant danger to life by capture, forced labor, or murder.

The journals of these fourteen young people (one identified only as "Anonymous Boy") from Germany, France, Poland, and the ghettos of Lodz, Kovno, Warsaw, and Terezin, carry stories across time, telling readers what these kids' days and hours were like, who they loved, who they lost—creating a portrait of hardships and heartbreak and danger and violence that few of us can fully imagine. There's also this: for these young writers, the diary wasn't just a place to document the wrenching events of their constantly threatened existence. Instead, the authors, even as they were writing in them, understood the journals as living things, and treated them as such. The stories were alive as long as the authors were; the creative act of writing provided meaning and purpose, and through this (and often only through this) the writers felt alive. This was not figurative; it was literal.

I chat on the phone with Alexandra, a writer and historian whom I've never met but whose work I've long admired, on a warm winter day in Palm Springs when Charlie is two years old. I hear Alexandra's kids moving in and out of rooms, a ball bouncing, a cabinet door closing, a dog barking. Charlie is watching *Mickey Mouse Clubhouse* with the volume turned low.

I ask Alexandra: "We know that objects in the natural world model resilience by their very nature, but is this a skill that can be learned? We talk about training our kids to be more resilient. Do you think the act of writing these journal entries and stories under unimaginable duress and threat to life made these children more resilient?"

Her answer? A flat-out no.

"Why?" I ask.

"Because," she continues, "to say we can learn to be resilient or teach people to be so presumes the power of agency, which is impossible to presume while living in a tyrannical state." In other words, resilience is not a set state or static quality one can aspire to or will oneself into. It is not a thing that can be *done* like an item to check off a list. Resilience is part of our human fabric, but only if we are considered human; only if we are treated as worthy of having life.

I ask Alexandra if during her research she noted or tracked any particular factors that made one journal writer more resilient than another. "It's like we think there's a recipe for ourselves and our children," I say, "to practice and hone resilience like a muscle. We keep hearing about the need to have 'grit' and to dig in to difficult circumstances." How does this change when people are actively trying to obliterate you and everyone you know? When every day brings a new threat of annihilation?

The concept of resilience is often approached through a kind of metrics: situation, commonalities, or particular, perhaps preexisting, character traits. There were no common components that made these children resilient. The world was utter chaos, so there were few common experiences at all, unless you count the daily promise of tumult and the threat of death. So many of the variables were external, dependent on a person's level of privilege and ability to be autonomous. Resilience, when a person must operate in survival mode, sometimes means only maintaining a sense of hope, or retaining enough sense of agency to write a paragraph about what happened that day; a belief that the documentation of the events of one's life still matters. It doesn't make sense to activate or acknowledge the power of brokenness if the world is hunting you down with the sole purpose of destroying you and everyone you love.

Ilya Gerber, one of the young writers in *Salvaged Pages,* was part of a privileged class in the ghetto. His father directed the Jewish Policeman's Chorus and was connected to the Jewish Council: this led to more food, more access to care and comfort, and a better chance of survival. Ilya still died. Does this mean he wasn't resilient, that he was a failure because he didn't activate his will in order to survive? As Alexandra says, "The big picture was not one in which he had any agency." Put simply, some circumstances are impossible to overcome. It means not that Ilya failed to "rise above" them, but that he lived under a regime entirely set on destroying him. We treat resilience as an aspirational goal, but when the world is so chaotic and so morally corrupt, resilience becomes a human right that, like life and the pursuit of it, no amount of money or willpower can secure. Resilience has conditions: it requires some sense of freedom, some modicum of safety to exist at all.

Given these realities, and the impact external circumstances have on a person's ability to *exist* in the world, does resilience have or did it have any meaning in the context of these children's lives? Yes, Alexandra believes, but it is not the meaning that has become part of the cultural vernacular. "Resilience in this context isn't about survival or living, it's not a quality one has; it's about living well while alive." What if we understood resilience as about *how* one lives, not whether or not one comes out being labeled a "survivor."

Alexandra tells me that the journal writers made it clear that *writing* was the path to maintaining any agency at all, which in this context *was life*. "People who are still writing are in touch with their agency. Claiming that identity enough to write something, they already have some resilience." And when life ceased to be livable, the writing stopped, and often the writer's life with it. "Some stopped writing in their diaries before they lost their lives. That silencing represents an inability to continue. Losing their voices is about losing something more."

Otto Wolf, the writer of the fifth diary in the book, stopped writing after he was captured; he died a few months later. His sister continued writing in the journal without identifying that she was the new author; only the change in handwriting signaled the change in authorship. The diary *became* her brother in some sense. "As long as the diary was being written, they were alive." It served, Alexandra tells me, as a way of being accounted for. If they didn't write in their diaries, they were not accounted for, as if they had simply disappeared. And yet, in the introduction to *Salvaged Pages*, Alexandra cautions the reader about projecting:

> The tragedy of a diary that survives its writer is not that we can read the text, come to know the writer in some concrete or abstract way, and grieve his or her death. Instead, the tragedy is that no surviving frag-

ment of genocide can reconstruct the person who created it; and that once dead, a person can never be known again. The essence in confronting the diaries in this book . . . is exactly *not* to confuse the reading of them with the rescue of individual lives, even symbolically, but to allow them to be seen as the partial records that they are; and to contemplate at one and the same time what is before us and what is lost and unrecoverable.

Alexandra explains how these young journal writers documented pain and suffering that was "so different from other forms of pain and suffering, because it was an existential threat. It wasn't like a terrible thing was happening to them, it was like [their] existence [was] threatened. The response to your existence being threatened is either you want to live versus . . . I'm in so much pain I want to die. And they also wanted to live. They wanted to come through it and have their lives again. Some did. Others didn't." For example, an anonymous boy in the Lodz ghetto writes on January 7, 1944 (in Polish): "I haven't had breakfast and I don't want to live any longer. I don't want to commit suicide but if I could cease existing in some painless way, if I could do this—I certainly would not hesitate"; and then, on July 6 of the same year, he writes in Hebrew: "I write these lines with anxiety and terrible grief—who knows what the next few days will bring us? Thousands have already been deported, tens of thousands more are going to be deported. In our present situation, when we have no strength left for walking on our feet, literally—

deportation is a mortal danger for us—even if they don't kill us right away, we will die from the hardships along the way—from starvation."

No amount of will, no amount of effort, no amount of trying can overcome some obstacles. Even in the face of these tyrannical forces, these impossible odds of survival, these children continued to want to live. Because that is what we want: to survive, to live. This wish is the cornerstone of resilience, but if you are starving, or sick, or both, you may be unable to survive, no matter how hard you try. This is not an individual's failure; it's the failure of hateful systems designed by hateful architects, intent on total destruction.

Tyranny produces no heroes. Terror dispenses no badges of bravery; it doesn't remove the desire to live, but it destroys the circumstances where living is possible. Tyranny can produce, in the case of these Holocaust diaries, "wretched fragments" that can teach us without inspiring us—they have neither that ability nor that tension. But both tyranny and terror can and do produce art. And in that process—necessary for these kids—lies life, for as long as it can be lived. The diary writers in *Salvaged Pages* responded to the utter chaos of life in the ghetto or in hiding with *stories*. To do creative work was to be—and feel—alive. "I believe that the project of living merits a response of some kind," Alexandra says. The need to be creative in the face of even the most profound destruction is a human impulse, a method of surviving that comes naturally. This doesn't make people brave, it makes them normal.

. . .

When I was nineteen, I visited the Holocaust Memorial Museum in Washington, D.C., during the time Alexandra Zapruder first began reading and editing the journals, but long before either of us became writers or knew each other. I walked through the museum, took notes, tried to process, to understand. Of course I knew that the Nazis' eugenic efforts extended to people with disabilities—Jews and non-Jews—and that people like me (and later, like Ronan) were murdered alongside GLBTQ people and gypsies and dissidents and Polish and Russian citizens. "Holocaust": in the thirteenth century, a wholly burnt offering or sacrifice by fire; from twelfth-century French, *holocauste*, and from Latin *holocaustum*, from Greek *holokauston*, a thing wholly burnt. *Holos*—whole, plus *kaustos*—from *kaiein*, to burn.

A room in one of the hallways displays the artificial legs taken from those who were murdered; again, there's no personalizing or contextualizing narrative to frame the objects we're encountering. The legs and braces are haphazardly collected, arranged to look as if they've just been tossed from the bodies that inhabited them, which was very likely what happened. The bodies of the legs are made of wood and metal, with variations in the color of the wood, ranging from pale beige (the color of my leg at the time), to light brown to dark brown to black. All have exoskeletal hinges and cloth waist straps—the latter once wrapped around a person's waist and absorbed their sweat and effort and blood. Many of the hinges are rust-stained, locked or cracked in permanent position. A fine layer of dust covers the foam feet.

At nineteen, I was still actively hiding my leg, which was made of the same materials that these legs—all of them with stories that would likely never be known held within them. I shook with fear and rage and confusion and even shame. It was like seeing a piece of my own body in that case of discarded parts of others' bodies. That delicate ankle. Those sculpted toes. These legs thought they were part of the body. They were not expecting to be preserved. I walked around the museum, trying to imagine the unimaginable, for what is imagination for if not to be recruited to try to understand what other humans may have felt or experienced in the last moments of their lives?

When I spoke with Alexandra, she talked about the struggle of the survivors who went on to live with the crushing knowledge that everything can fall away without reason or warning. There's life, yes, but there's another reality just behind it. She told me, "They know that nothing is a sure thing and you don't get a do-over." No matter how hard you try. No matter how much you might want one. This knowledge provides insight, but little comfort, and perhaps that is as it should be.

In 2016, physician Siddhartha Mukherjee would publish *The Gene: An Intimate History,* and in it he would speculate about whether resilience has a "genetic core." He would document the search by scientists for a "resilience gene," named so after a study called the Strong African American Families Program, in an impoverished area of rural Georgia plagued by crime, violence, alcoholism, and drug use. Scientists wondered if an individual's genetics might affect their chances of surviving this difficult landscape. Local families were tested for the variant of the gene 5-HTTLPR. The short variant had been linked to individuals more prone to alcoholism and mental illness. The long variant was linked with "normality."

The study showed that those with the short variant of the gene were more likely to binge-drink, use drugs, and be sexually permissive. Together with an impoverished and potentially violent upbringing, this "bad" gene seemed a predictor for a terrible life; none of this was a surprise. But the researchers didn't stop there; they offered counseling to those with both the short variant and the long variant. Those in the short-variant group, the ones more genetically prone to behaviors that would hinder an escape from a grim future, were more open to counseling than those in the long-variant group.

And thus the idea of a resilience gene was born, leading some psychologists to suggest that the "short-variant" children who might exhibit behavior problems should be particularly targeted (at great cost) for intervention, because they are more receptive, genetically, to assistance. Mukherjee points out the problematic ethics of any such plan; if children are genotyped as having a greater propensity toward "resilience," then those in power can decide who gets educational dollars, services, and resources, and who does not.

It may sound like a scenario from a science fiction film, but Mukherjee points out that we've been here before. The renaissance of "gene profiling" and categorizing children (and, essentially, ranking their worth on a deliberate and brutalizing ladder) is analogous to the "Nazi program to cleanse the 'genetically sick' that resulted in the deaths of millions." He goes on to argue that "the dehumanization of the mentally ill and the physically disabled ('they cannot think or act like us') was a warp act to the dehumanization of Jews ('they don't think or act like us'). Never before in history, and never with such insidiousness, had genes been so effortlessly conflated with identity, identity with defectiveness, and defectiveness with extermination."

On that day when I was nineteen at the Holocaust museum, I didn't know what unknown variants I carried in my genes; that inherited story that would lead to the story of a lost child had not yet been disclosed to me, nor had the story of a living child who would grow up after and alongside it. On that day when I was nineteen, I walked and walked through the crowded museum halls. I looked and looked and tried to see. To feel. My whole body felt like it was on fire. The legs behind glass before me and my leg were both made of wood, that resilient material meant to withstand torque and abuse; meant to shift with movement and weight; meant to warp as a way of recovering. Unless a match is set to it. Then it will quickly and easily burn.

CHAPTER TWELVE

March

We stand at the prow again of a small ship
anchored late at night in the tiny port
looking over to the sleeping island: the waterfront
is three shuttered cafés and one naked light burning.
To hear the faint sound of oars in the silence as a rowboat
comes slowly out and then goes back is truly worth
all the years of sorrow that are to come.

JACK GILBERT, FROM "A BRIEF FOR THE DEFENSE"

It is much more uncomfortable to drive up to the mesa behind our house in New Mexico while nine months pregnant than it is to run up it; the unpaved road is cluttered with
rocks and boulders and potholes that a foot might step around
but that a tire can easily get lost in. I sit in the front of the
truck with my friend Anne, a photographer who took beautiful pictures of Ronan while he was living and who has asked
me to be part of a new photo series based on the Tarot deck.
"Do you want to be the Empress?" she asks me. I do. Who
wouldn't? It's March 1, and I'm a little over a week away from
my C-section date. We go slowly, but my teeth are still rattling when I try to talk.

Once on top of the mesa, I show Anne where I've buried some of Ronan's hair. I take off my clothes and let her assistant wrap me in sheer blue and red and purple clothes. She puts a gold crown on my head.

"The Empress in the deck," Anne says from behind the camera, "is someone very powerful." The sun is warm against my bare shoulders, but the air is crisp and bites a bit. I feel silly at first, but then I get into it. Below me the desert is dotted with green shrubs; in the distance, the mountains look like intricately cut paper shapes that have been glued to the blue sky. When I see the photographs for the first time, it looks like the top of my head is touching the single cloud floating high above it. I end up as the High Priestess from the Tarot deck, on a panel that is nearly ten feet tall, but on that bright, chilly morning, carrying life as well as the memory of death, I don't care who I will play in the deck. I care only that I'm alive.

Nineteen forty-four. March in central Illinois, a place where the flat land makes an even seam with the sky in every direction. That afternoon it might have been unseasonably warm, or the ground might still have been frozen, with thin islands of ice cracking under his footfall. Maybe the fresh smell of mud hung in the air; maybe the stiff, bright smell of snow. My grandfather, thirty-five, broad-shouldered, at six feet four the tallest man in town, the only one with the thick red hair he was known by, walked to the barn where he kept the oil trucks he drove to fuel the farming equipment in the area. He took his shotgun off the wall and shot himself in the mouth. Inside the house on the other side of the lawn, my mother was eighteen months old, her brother nearly four years old. My grandmother was not yet thirty; she would live for only another twenty years, dying of heart disease that was a result of having contracted scarlet fever as a child.

Over seven decades later, I'm in the small Southern California town where I live, having breakfast with my mom at a cozy café that plays religious country music and serves pancakes the size of your head, when she slides a photograph of her mother across the table. "Now *that's* a resilient woman," she says. "Since you're writing about resilience." Outside the December weather is not so dissimilar to what it will likely still be in March: temperate, sunny, largely windless.

In the photograph, taken in the late 1930s, my grandmother is wearing a wool coat that hangs to her ankles and a tilted beret over dark hair cut in a short bob; her hands are tucked into a fur muff that matches the collar of her coat. She is tiny, a little over five feet tall, and looks even smaller standing beneath the tree in front of the house where she would be sleeping or perhaps brewing coffee, or perhaps writing a letter, not so many years later, on the day her husband killed himself. She is smiling. Her shoulders are shrugged up in imitation of a flirty, silent movie star pose. Her face is a copy of my mother's face. As a child I used to pull open the heavy wooden drawer of my parents' bedside table, open the slim blue box where pictures of my grandmother were housed, and stare at them for hours, as if this could help me know her.

When I had my DNA tested after Ronan's diagnosis, all the strands pulled apart like string cheese and analyzed, I learned that I have Moroccan ancestry, and that my Tay-Sachs mutation is the most ancient variation; when I found information about Moroccan Jewish communities online, I scrolled through photographs of women who look just like the image of my grandmother that my mother is showing me now. My parents have not been tested for Tay-Sachs, although one of them must be a carrier. "I don't want to know," my mom maintains. "I don't want to feel guilty."

My grandmother didn't choose to be sick; she didn't choose to be a widow with two small children. She did choose to love her children, to seek happiness, to laugh. "She was my person," my mom always said. "I told her everything, and even if she didn't approve, she never judged me."

Nobody ever talked about my grandfather; my mother did not discover he died by suicide until she was in her twenties, while she was in nursing school. People postulated, of course, about what had "been wrong"—gambling debts, alcoholism, mental illness—but no definitive information supported any of these speculations.

One afternoon when my mom was ten years old, she realized her mother became terribly winded as they were walking up the few stairs to the dentist's office. "She smiled at me and ruffled my hair and said, 'Don't worry; nothing a bit of ice cream can't fix.'" She made all the dresses my mother wore to her high school dances; she went on all the crash diets my mom experimented with in the fifties (grapefruit, popcorn, fasting), and then took Mom to the ice cream parlor when her willpower gave out. "All the time she was working as a nurse as a single mom—a total rarity in our community and at that time—she always came home with a smile on her face, waiting to hug us," my mom told me. "Even though our financial situation and her health were precarious, we felt safe."

Although it was a risky surgery, my grandmother chose to be the first patient in Illinois to have a heart valve replaced with a valve from a pig's heart, which bought her another decade with her kids. Her heart gave out a few weeks after my parents' wedding in August 1967, when she died in my mother's arms. "She never wanted to die alone," my mom said, "and she didn't."

"She was no saint, though," my mom says. "She wasn't afraid to be angry, but she was never cruel, and she was never bitter. She was honest about her frailty, but she worked with it. When the other moms were swimming with their kids at our little watering hole, Patty's Pond, she'd come, too, only she'd sit under an umbrella and read *Ladies' Home Journal.* She may have been dealt a crap hand, but she played it beautifully. She hated it when people said she was brave."

"What did she think she was?"

My mom takes a sip of coffee, looks at me, and says, "Just living."

CHAPTER THIRTEEN

King of the Road

A vole darts over the surface, black and elegant.
In a vast theater: one note played on a piano.
It vanishes under a drift.

Briefly the trees hold the light in their arms.

JENNY GEORGE, FROM "WINTER VARIATIONS"

When Ronan is dying, my dad tells me a story about his favorite mentor in seminary, Pastor Kirsons, who was dying in 1965, during my dad's final year of graduate school. My dad and Kirsons's Latvian friends took turns sitting with him and drinking vodka in the small Chicago apartment he shared with his wife, Rasma, who like Kirsons had grown up in the Latvian colony of Ufa, Russia. After World War II, they were displaced persons who eventually traveled to the United States. My father, who had no father figure of his own, admired and respected Kirsons immensely.

Seminarians loved their cookouts, Dad tells me, lots of bratwursts and beer, and during one of those afternoons, as others were preparing the food and setting the table, my dad was with Kirsons and could see he was in pain. He listened to the meat sizzle on the grill in the yard, felt his mouth water with hunger as he smelled it through the open window. He felt embarrassed and helpless and stupid.

"Then," he says, "I watched him look over the Eisenhower Expressway that ran parallel to the seminary, and he noticed flowers behind a white picket fence on the other side. He said, 'Look, I see flowers. I think they are roses.' I looked, but could see nothing. I think he was the only one who saw them."

That summer while Kirsons was dying, my dad worked in the refectory, and the song "King of the Road" by Roger Miller was a huge hit. Dad used to sing it while scraping scalloped potato rinds from the cooking pans. He tells me he hated it when this dish was served because the entire time he was eating them he knew what a bitch it would be to clean the pans later. "Trailer for sale or rent/room to rent fifty cents./No home, no school, no pet/I ain't got no cigarettes."

"Whenever I hear that song," Dad says, "I think of a day in mid-June when I was sitting with Kirsons. His breathing was labored, and clearly he was miserable. He said to me, 'I want to get it over with as soon as possible.'"

Then on a horribly hot day near the end of August, just before fall classes began, my dad was taking his turn with Kirsons, reading a book now because conversation was out of the question. By this time Kirsons had lost consciousness and was breathing slowly, and then his breathing stopped. He was fifty-two years old. My dad stepped into the small living room, and Rasma looked at him and immediately knew what had happened. They said a prayer together. On the wall was a small crucifix, and my dad cursed it, using every bit of profanity he knew (under his breath, of course); he was so angry that this man who had so much to offer, and who was still so young, was gone.

My dad tells me that all of this happened at a time when he was "young and stupid, a scrawny country boy who thought faith could be about love or about fear, but not about both." When he'd been sitting at his mentor's bedside, he'd told Kirsons that he no longer believed in God, not after what was happening to him. Kirsons became visibly angry and said, "We don't know and we can't ask why."

"Now," my dad tells me, "when I look at Ronan I am asking why."

Decades after my father witnessed his mentor's death and he and my mother together had witnessed my grandmother's, my parents record a book for Ronan into the belly of a soft bear: *On the Night You Were Born*. At the end of the book, which they read, alternating line by line, my dad says in a strangled voice, "We love you, Ronan. Sweet boy. Love you all the time." Sometimes I'll be putting Charlie's toys away and accidentally touch the bear's tummy. Suddenly I hear the story read aloud in the bright pink of Charlie's play room and I'll think of the day Ronan died, my dad in the yard, looking up, saying, "I think that's a robin on the branch. Can you see him?" And then, two years later, pointing out an eagle to Charlie as it sails over the yard and then beyond, the brightness of the white tail lingering until it is gone from view. Both moments, and perhaps all the moments any of us can have, live in the line from the poem "Intelligence" by Jenny George: "happiness with its horizon of pain."

CHAPTER FOURTEEN

The Panic Room

The hole goes down and down.
It has many rooms
like graves and like graves
they are all connected.

JENNY GEORGE, FROM "ORIGINS OF VIOLENCE"

Less than a month after Ronan died, I'm off on a book tour for *The Still Point of the Turning World,* a book that ends with my son still alive in its pages. Now everything is different, everything has changed, and each night brings a new city and the same rolling bag packed with the same dresses and shoes: hipster hotel rooms in Houston and San Francisco where guests can request a fish delivered to the room as a "pet for the night" to stave off loneliness; a generic Marriott in Chicago; a sleek Hilton in Denver, where the closets are made of mirrors. I struggle to sleep, and am usually on a treadmill at 5:00 A.M. and then again at 5:00 P.M., wherever I am. I do cellphone interviews in taxis to and from the airport with various magazine editors. I do a television interview that I have not watched and never will watch. I watch episodes of *Law & Order: SVU* on repeat until I fall asleep; there's almost always another episode playing on the same station when I wake up, sometimes the same one. I have dreams that the lead actress, Mariska Hargitay, and I are friends, and I'm so sleep deprived that I'm convinced I see her at a reading one evening.

People are gracious, and the crowds vary from embarrassingly small (a woman piping up, asking, "Are you the cookbook author?") to surprisingly large and lively. The question-and-answer part of the reading is always my favorite part until it isn't.

"You must have a cold heart," one woman in an audience somewhere suggests, "since you are able to talk about your son to all of these strangers without crying." My son hasn't been dead for a month. Her words land and lodge in my throat—*you have a cold heart*—and for a moment I'm unable to speak. It's such a cruel thing to say, such an outrageous accusation, that it takes me a few long moments to formulate a response. I tell her that if I allowed myself to feel what I felt in those cold morning hours of Ronan's death, I would not be able to do anything; I would be unable to take a single step forward. As I talk, I'm growing angrier and angrier, sweat popping at my hairline. "There are only a few people who can go to that place with me," I say evenly, "and none of them are in this room." She opens and closes her mouth. I sign all the books in a furious silence, hardly looking up.

For the next few days I'm unable to shake that woman's words, or to get out from under her proclamation, which feels like a solid character judgment.

Carl Jung imagined retreating into a room as a way of escaping from trauma. He writes, "The unbearable pain of a particular traumatic event that went on for a few days was replaced by another sensation: something happened that I had observed in myself several times before: there was a sudden inner silence, as though a soundproof door had been closed on a noisy room."

Who can open that door? I think of the room as a hole, the way Jenny George describes it in "Origins of Violence":

> *Roots hang from the dirt*
> *in craggy chandeliers.*
> *It's warm and dark down there.*
> *The passages multiply.*
> *There are ballrooms.*
> *There are dead ends.*
> *The air smells of iron and*
> *crushed flowers.*

The hole drops and drops, getting deeper and deeper, creating spaces and rooms a griever can drop into or explore, unwillingly, at any moment of any day. And sometimes the hole is a crypt suddenly filled with light and fresh air, as if someone has thrown open a window on a summer morning before the heat of the day descends and all the curtains are closed to trap in the cool air.

At an interdisciplinary dinner at my university, I meet a physicist who specializes in dark matter, the stuff of the universe we can't see or prove, he explains, but that scientists believe makes our lives possible. "I love my family and we're

all here except Ronan," Charlie says one night before bed-
time. The ability to disconnect in those moments, to trap and
somehow contain the howl in the panic room, makes it possible for me to connect. I touch her head through the dark
matter of the air that has within it the energy of Ronan and
everyone else who has lived and loved and say, "Yes, that's
right." Ronan's body and Charlie's body; her first day and his
last; Charlie's hand in mine each day and the plaster cast of
Ronan's; one love lost and another gained.

My panic room is no longer a place of such tornado-like
sadness, although sometimes it can be. More often than not,
it feels like a cool cave of bereavement, a solid resting place,
not the loud, driving-on-the-rumble-strip feeling of grief at
its highest octave. The truth is that grief never lessens, it just
moves around, and for me, and I think for many others, it
moves around in a room that itself changes shape: a square, a
well, a hole in a cracking wall, the corner of a sweltering
attic, the aching belly of a hungry animal. A scream might
be hiding in the wallpaper. The creak of the floorboards
might shift into a hurricane; the memory of a baby's sigh
might shake the room into the shape of a crib or a net or a
boat, rocking the griever, tossing them into an ocean made of
quicksand. In the same way I can't see dark matter, I cannot
see my panic room, but I have proof of its existence each
time I unwittingly feel a drop—or a descent—into each new
shape or iteration.

CHAPTER FIFTEEN

The Art of Bearing Witness

The moon shines down from the black November sky.
The tide rises like a sweeping, white-ruffed arm,
erasing all the pages that have come before.
The evidence accumulates that nobody is watching over us,

and gradually, as the streets and houses drift toward night,
all the words inside them close their eyes;
the sentences coil up like snakes and sleep.

It's just me now and my famous aching heart
under the stars—my heart that keeps moving like a searchlight
in its longing for the hearts of other people,
who, in a sense, already live there, in my heart,

and keep it turning.

TONY HOAGLAND, FROM "A WALK AROUND THE PROPERTY"

When I began writing about Ronan and my grief experience in a very public blog format, beavering away on essays long into the night, my former college religion professor, Barbara, responded to every single one. Her husband was worried, she wrote, that reading my posts and peering so deeply into another's despair would upset her. "How does one negotiate the relationship between that which we know and that which we choose to tell?" she wondered. But, she went on, "Reading for me is just sitting and listening and silently just being there." When I had my son, in March 2010, Barbara was one of the first to congratulate me. When he was diagnosed she wrote me a letter—handwritten, on a sheet from a white legal pad. For the next two and a half years, Barbara wrote me regular, sometimes weekly, letters, remarkable letters that were revealing, loving, and kind. Honest. Full of rage and searching.

She talked about the biblical Job and the way his friends were helpful to him in his great trials until they opened their mouths and tried to explain and rationalize his despair. "It all seems a terrible mistake, all this darkness," she continued. "It must be; but here I'm in danger of starting to question, to rationalize, and that won't help. Just know that I am thinking of you, sitting, and listening." She promised to keep doing so, and she kept that promise.

Barbara's letters were not just about my work and what was happening with my son but about her life as well. At first she worried about discussing the family vacation and the events of her daily life because she didn't want to bore me, or hurt me, or make me feel jealous. But I wanted to know, I wrote back. I wanted to peer into the life of someone whose family wasn't falling apart, whose children weren't dying, in part because I knew she didn't pity me, she was walking with me, in the age-old tradition of Ruth and Naomi, although we shared no familial tie.

She sent me book reviews, reports about her latest theological interests, the copy of a check she had written me for babysitting services ($54.86, dated May 1996—"We were so cheap!"), and one rollicking discussion from "a summer in full swing," about what the sixteenth-century Protestant theologian John Calvin might say about luck. "Death won't be the end," she wrote, and I sensed in her a desire to believe this, even if she didn't, not quite. Another letter was in visibly shaky handwriting, composed during a turbulent plane ride.

Through our exchanges, I began to realize that I hadn't really known Barbara at all—not until now—when she revealed more about herself than she ever had. I was no longer young, foolishly believing that possibilities were endless. Our correspondence signaled an adult awareness of mortality, that death is always closer than we think.

The summer before Ronan's death, the summer I stood on the bridge and thought about jumping, she wrote, "I'm sending you lots of love and positive thoughts. Hope you feel it." I did, and I do. Yes, we had decades of shared history behind us, but now we had truly gotten to know and love one another as women, thinkers, and mothers. Equals. This switch from youthful adoration to a more nuanced relationship included an element of loss.

The last letter, written right before Ronan died, was the most personal and perhaps the most profound. I realized, reading it, that this exchange of ideas had altered us both, earned us each other's trust in a new and radical way. She told me the story about her daughter Maggie's birth, one that would never have been included in a mass email announcement. After Maggie was born and she was taken away to be cleaned and weighed before returning to her mother, a nurse arrived to take care of Barbara, to wash and comfort her. "Time seemed to stop," she wrote, "and this moment in which the flow of time seemed to be completely suspended, my thought was this: this is a baptism, and this is the moment when I become a parent, this is the anointing."

Barbara went on to say that she believed my experience of parenting a terminally ill child had made me a better person, not in a superficial, moralistic sense. "I think he's made you better by opening up the great fire of your love," she wrote, with his "small but magnificent existence." I have never in my life read a more deeply comforting sentence, one that spoke to my grandest hopes, my deepest fears, and the only faith that remains to me, which is a belief in chaos.

Mentors are tasked with ushering those in their charge into fresh understanding, new perceptions; they are meant to help those who have placed trust in them learn how to sort and filter new experiences, or assist in the project of making sense out of the mess that is human life, or at least doggedly ask questions that dig deep toward those difficult and nuanced answers. Mentoring is a sacred relationship with ancient roots; I envision it as a loving recognition, a way of saying "I see you; I'm here." Unlike Job's friends, who want to sort and solve, mentors witness. They observe and accompany the darkest despair, the wildest sorrow, and the most unexpected joy. My mentor first taught me to love my mind, and later, when the life of the mind she had helped me develop was the only way to withstand and survive the thunderous days with my dying child, she wrote me letters that stood witness to my life, in all its wretchedness and joy, in all its terrible beauty. When I was a child, the image of WALK

BESIDE ME, AND JUST BE MY FRIEND, which I had seen first on the banner in the church basement, set for me a template for expectation about friendships, exquisitely realized here in my adulthood.

When I was four years old, about six months after my leg was amputated, my family drove to central Illinois, where my parents grew up and where my uncle and aunt and three cousins still lived. During those hot and humid summers, everyone went to the water park, but I had not yet been fitted with an artificial limb, was still on crutches, and could not climb the stairs to any slides. My cousin Kate, then ten years old, was mortified that I would be left out, so she offered to carry me. And she did. She carried me on her back up the stairs to the water slide, hour after hour, for three days straight. I remember the sweet, processed smell of Banana Boat sunscreen and how she felt as she carried me—wet, warm, the muscles tensing and releasing under my chest. The strain she was willing to endure to gift me with an experience I would never have had otherwise is an act of kindness and effort that has stayed with me all my life.

We carry one another, in whatever ways we can. When people ask: Can trauma make you better? Isn't it true that what doesn't kill you makes you stronger? No. What doesn't kill you changes you, and those who choose to love you. That is what it means to bear witness, a unique and salvific form of resilience.

CHAPTER SIXTEEN

City of Grief

What I thought were graves
from this height are houses
in neat white rows. In the absence
of faith I resort to magical
thinking. I pray to my children,
which is to say I conjure them,
imagine holding them until
I can feel them in my arms.
Like a sign that dings on, lit:
Mother. *Though motherhood*
never kept anyone safe.
Just a week ago, an opera singer
held her baby on her lap
as a mountain chewed their plane
to bits. How is that possible?
Didn't the mountain see the baby?
Motherhood never kept anyone
safe, though it's no fault of mothers.

MAGGIE SMITH, FROM "ROUGH AIR"

Just like turbulence, you never know when it will hit you, make your thought luggage tumble from the overstuffed overhead bins of your mind. Reminders of who or what you've lost can be hidden in the unlikeliest of places, ready to puncture the thin veil that separates you from your grief, like the veil that separates your lived life from an imagined life or memories of the past. A single red mitten found in a drawer, tucked under condolence cards you've neglected to throw out or save or frame; a photo that slips from the pages of a book you read years ago, confronting you with the face of the person you've lost, perhaps even a swooping sample of their handwriting in a birthday card; a stray song lyric that floats in from a neighbor's car at a stoplight and knocks you back in time. It can happen anytime, anywhere, and unless you're constantly vigilant, which is no way to live, grief crashes into you when you least expect it. It kicks you awake and suddenly you feel like you have the heart flu, or that you've been crying for days even though your eyes are dry.

Each summer I visit my friends Rebecca and Justin at their home in the Berkshire Mountains in Western Massachusetts. Rebecca and I met through our different experiences of bereavement. The cofounder of Modern Loss, an intentionally judgment-free community dedicated to open communication about all the complications surrounding grief, she has become one of my closest friends. As we like to say, grief gives mostly shit gifts, but sometimes it gives you people you may never have met otherwise, and whom you grow to love. Now we do readings and retreats and live storytelling events that Rebecca spectacularly plans and produces to sold-out bookstore audiences in Brooklyn; at Edith Wharton's historic estate in Lenox, Massachusetts; at the Kripalu retreat center, where we get Tarot card readings, meet two incredible adaptive yoga teachers, and at some point realize we are the only people not wearing designer yoga pants. Charlie loves to play with Rebecca and Justin's boys, and they welcome me like a sister, setting up picnic and live music dates at Tanglewood and opening their best bottles of red wine for dinners on the deck. I love their house in the trees, and I love them. If I could, I would buy a house next door without a second thought.

I arrive one summer night around midnight, having driven from Albany on a series of dark, steamy country roads with a still and watchful canopy of lush green trees stretching overhead for the final few miles. I drive slowly up the gravel driveway with the headlights off and walk slowly across the lawn and through the door, which I close carefully because their baby, Eliot, sleeps in the nursery directly above this room; he's a light sleeper and any slamming door might roust him.

As I'm tiptoeing through the mudroom, I trip over a shoe. Before I hit the floor and give the whole house a crash-landing wake-up call, I steady myself on a bike handle and look up. There, balanced on a pile of Amazon boxes and crates stuffed with outgrown boys' clothes, as if about to spring upward, is Ronan's identical bouncer: the red parrot he tried to bat with his soft hand when he still had volitional movement; the blue lizard with yellow spots that spun so easily inside the plastic egg attached to one part of the bouncer's circle; a few colored birds hanging from the green canopy on the circle's opposite side. I liked to call him DJ Rones. Of course it's not actually Ronan's bouncer, it's simply the same model, but it's as if this object has conjured him completely, and all the emotions that come with his absence: sadness, numbness, guilt, love, ache, guilt again. A tumble of feelings

that don't register fully before connecting with those that follow. As Charlie likes to say when a plane hits turbulence:
"My brain hurts." My brain registers what feels like an insult, and also my heart, which feels like it's burrowing into
my body, seeking to self-protect.

Without thinking, I feel Ronan's weight in my arms when
I thought he was healthy and I maneuvered him out of that
bouncer's red cloth seat; and then the weight of his wasted
body, so thin and fragile and tiny, as if all the flesh had been
lifted away, when I placed him in the undertaker's kind and
waiting arms. At the same time I can feel Charlie's squirmy
and spry little body when I dry her off after a bath. I see her
pale lashes darkened by water, and the impossible freckles
scattered perfectly across her nose and cheeks. These visceral
memories collide instantly. I often talk to my writing students about the necessity of two things happening at once, or
the principle of simultaneity, and the importance of layering
in essays and scenes. But all I can think now is that this is bad
timing for a grief trigger or a sprained ankle in a friend's
basement, and I'm grateful that I haven't made any noise.

It's only 9:00 P.M. in California, so I lie in the guest room,
wide awake, listening to the bugs just beyond the windows
pulse their soothing night rhythms and regretting the giant
Dunkin' Donuts coffee I gulped down at the Albany airport
to be sure I arrived here safely; or, more accurately, to be sure
I stayed awake just in case I got lost and the trip took longer
than it should, and so I am awake in the dark, my friends and
their children and their dog asleep in the rooms above me. I
am filled with a weird worry for their vulnerable sleeping
bodies, the way I often feel about my students when they

come in with their ideas and their essays and say, "I'm afraid I'm no good," as they're sitting on the other side of my desk, and I immediately imagine my students asleep, which is one way of being fully alone. Imagining them (or anyone) this way—so isolated, so vulnerable—helps me feel compassion, because I find this statement that is actually a rhetorical question tedious, irritating, and, of course, normal, as I ask it of myself frequently. Who am I to be so impatient?

And yet I am. Impatient with these memories of Ronan and Charlie held together like two parts of a single life, or one part each of two lives, and this moment of two *lives*, two *children* being conjured at once makes me feel edgy and broken and damaged. I will my roving thoughts to land on something tangible, something *thinkable*, the solace of the bereaved—a task, any task—and eventually they do.

In 1998, while I'm living in Geneva and working for a Christian relief organization, I start experiencing what is known as "compassion fatigue," a frequent phenomenon for those who do relief work. There is so much struggle and death and horror all over the world; the civil war in Sierra Leone had resulted in thousands of amputees with no access to medical care or rehabilitation; babies died after antibiotics were stolen at a border; HIV/AIDS was spreading too quickly for even the most robust prevention programs to halt it.

One morning in the office, after receiving an email about another civil war and how the organization was appropriating funds to serve those affected, I realize I am numb. I stub out my cigarette (everyone smoked in their offices then), and

I walk across the hall to tell my co-worker, Ana, that I'm not experiencing the emotions I used to have—outrage, sadness, grief—when I began this work; instead, I feel nothing.

"Silent meditation is the answer!" she insists, and shows me the location of Taizé, an ecumenical monastery in eastern France, on our office map.

"Two days is all you need, in my experience," she says. "It gets you straight back to your heart."

That sounds like the perfect thing to "reset," as Ana says, so I call and enroll in a silent weekend retreat, which I am excited about until the day before; I feel my enthusiasm for silence winnowing as the road south narrows and turns to gravel, and especially when the chartered bus drops us off with the brothers in the main house, who remind us of the rules: NO TALKING. I listen carefully to the brother's instructions; he wears a plain brown cloak and looks about my age, early twenties. "We eat and drink silently as a way of honoring God," he says. That night I lie awake in my top bunk, blinking into the darkness, listening to the breath of the strangers sleeping around me.

I zone out during Bible study, but enjoy the walks through the nearby woods that Jews escaping Nazi-occupied France once ran through to reach the safety that Brother Roger provided here—a sanctuary. Brother Roger is thin, pale, and slightly bent by age. He has a soft voice and is very calm, moving very little. When he speaks his hands stay folded in front of him on the table.

I lose my interest pretty quickly in the absence of words or speech. The world begins to feel like a paper cutout of itself, all the edges too prominent and precise, as if the scenes could be easily folded up together. *Fold here, here, and here and there's the world in your pocket, small enough to simply throw away.* An origami world: perfectly constructed, so easy to crush. I am angry at myself for taking my precious vacation days to say nothing to anyone when I might have been reading on a white beach in Greece or drinking cheap, delicious wine in Italy. Couldn't that have helped me access the inner workings of my heart?

Each morning the French Girl Scouts air-greet one another with kisses in the frigid bathrooms, a sound that feels as loud as applause inside the silence, the crisp white collars of their uniforms twitching. Footsteps over frozen snow sound like gunfire. I feel morbid and mortal, which I suppose is the idea. We are supposed to be growing closer to God, our maker and our eventual undertaker; it is meant to be uncomfortable, and it is. I am less and less convinced of any belief or piety as the hours wear silently on. If there had been a pay phone within walking distance of this monastery, I would have been living in it, using whatever money I had to call whomever I could reach and just *talk*.

The only respite offered is the prayer singing session each night; I've never before been so excited about singing Latin chants in a room full of strangers. The large metal cross in the center of the dark room, covered in candles with skinny flames that waver and snap, seems to float. We sing the same Kyrie over and over, on endless repeat, swaying side to side— mourning, it seems, for something that cannot be named because it cannot be spoken aloud. People cry and shift in their seats, pleading, *Jesus Jesus remember me remember me* in every language.

Seven years later, in 2005, a young Romanian woman will stroll through the candlelit meditation room during the evening prayers and stab Father Roger in the heart. He will die moments later.

Taizé, the village of silence, grieving penitents longing for relief. Did they find it? No way to know.

When I return to the office, Ana asks me how I feel, how it went.

"I don't know," I say. "It's like I'm wearing a shell or something. I was hoping to feel more opened up."

"Ah," she says, and smiles. "Now you will feel everything again for the first time when the shell breaks."

Now, decades later, trying to fall asleep in a small town near different mountains, immersed in a different kind of silence, I'm stuck on this idea of the city of grief: the place you go after yours or a loved one's diagnosis, or after a person has died, or when you're waiting for someone to die.

At first, it's a lonely place, dark and terrifying. You're sure there are dangerous snakes and all manner of monsters lying in wait. You're naked, of course, and either too cold or too hot, and you are alone. The air smells of rot and shit and clothes that will never fully dry. You can make out no shadows of buildings or discernible walkways. There's a storm coming; you can feel the dangerous shift in the breeze and the tell of thunder in the distance. You wail and cry and hope someone throws you a rope so you can climb out. I know that place well; I lived in it for years.

But then, like all cities do, my grief city changed. The

light poured in again. The roads and alleyways were no longer crumbling and full of potholes: people navigated clean, shiny bikes through rain-washed streets, wearing smiles or looks of concentration; fresh-faced and friendly-looking strangers were reading books in tree-filled parks that had sprung up overnight; and when the seasons changed, nobody died.

It's one o'clock in the morning now, and I need to distract my thoughts into rest if possible. We're about to run a three-day grief retreat, and I know that other people's stories of loss can be such heavy lifting, so much to hold. I try to imagine what my grief city is like at this moment in time, and it comes to me instantly and without effort; the images are so comforting, the place so soothing, that it's the last thing I remember before falling asleep.

On this day in my grief city it is autumn. In the middle of the city is a lake, and my maternal grandmother and grandfather stand in the shallow end wearing nineteenth-century swimming suits and splashing water on each other. Light falls through the drops of water, scattering rainbows over their bare white feet. Both of them have perfect hair—Grandma's a short cut from the 1920s; Grandpa's styled in a stiff wave over his giant forehead. I never met my mother's parents, but here they are, and they know me and I know them. The lake glimmers with shadows from the sun that cuts through the leaves, which are red and orange and bright green, the colors of a Boston fall. And there is Ronan, running in and out of the lake, away from the waves, laughing. His hair flips up behind his ears like little wings. He is carefree and at ease in his body in this world, and so am I, seeing him this way. This is more than anyone, I suppose, could ask for. If I believed in heaven, I would wish for it to have this ease, this lightness, this rare simplicity of being.

The rest of the city consists of a few houses made of a light, strong wood set haphazardly in a stand of aspen trees. Inside, each house has a ladder leading to a loft, where there's a lightly whirring fan, a bed with a soft blanket, and a light to read by. In every house there is a fireplace that is easy to light. Stars are always visible through the windows after night falls.

A train runs high up along the ridge of this little hollow city of grief, multicolored cars that twist and wind and create a rumbling sound that feels like an intermittent lullaby at night. There is a cathedral at one end of the single street. It is made of gray stone, Irish style, with an old graveyard full of Celtic crosses. But the graves are decorated with balloons and toys, and food is left there to feed the hungry dead.

Every morning the priests, young and old, walk down the hill into the town to talk to the people—just to be with them, just to remind them that they are not alone, will never be alone—and they wear long, pale blue robes that swish around their ankles as they move. Their heavy silver crosses hanging on long chains swing over their chests, back and forth with each forward step, a mobile blessing. One priest is always last, and that's Ronan, too, and when he turns to look at me I see, for just a moment, the face he never grew to have, the faded freckles across his nose and cheeks, and then he turns away and keeps walking, falling in step with the others.

CHAPTER SEVENTEEN

It's a Good Thing the Body Is So Smart

And so I was scared to be in my body,
in the same way one fears a particular house.
. . .

Yet my body extends itself outward—
it is now the house, the rooftop, the lake and lotus—

this is not good news, is not beauty:
I am everywhere and the fear, when it desires
to grow, grows continental, drifting,
torn, submerged—

and so I ask my body for another house.

But the body worsens under the extremity of the request,
saddening further like corners
of a fabric sack
bearing the very most of the stones.
. . .

From my bed I lay repeating
to the mute and early morning, I am not
the house, I am
not the house, I
am not a house.

KATIE FORD, FROM "IN THE HEARTH"

At the Kripalu retreat center in Western Massachusetts, where I'm leading a grief retreat with Rebecca, writer and founder of Modern Loss, and Christine, a pro cyclist, writer, and cycling instructor with Peloton, the wildly popular indoor cycling company, I convene a small discussion group that I jokingly refer to as "body shit."

"Come on down to body shit," I say. "We all have it!" The goal is to share with others the myriad ways in which grief lands in a person's body, and how it stays there, and what that means for identity, which in turn influences decision making. Grief lights a fire under all of these trajectories, crisscrossing like jet streams in the sky and just as quickly dissolving. Just as grief reorders your emotional life, it rearranges your physical body. The long-term and lasting effects of this disordering in the body are vast and deep, I believe, and often dramatically underestimated. In Jenny George's "Dream of Reason," these lines—"Each day the same/scandal—this body"—is a poetic way of saying "body shit."

I use a friendly, lighthearted tone in my "pitch" to bring people to the group, but it turns out they come anyway. The fact that we carry grief in our bodies and the way in which we carry it are no joke. We do all have it.

There are so many stories. Worries about gaining weight or making money don't stop when a person you love is suffering or dying. The body understands, even if the mind does not: Some people broke out in hives or boils, as if the grief wanted to work its way out of the skin. I remember my friend Lucy, after her husband died, refusing to leave the hospital; her mind could not process the fact that he had died, although she'd been his doctor and caretaker for two years. The body: It's smart. But it can tolerate only so much.

To the group I admit being surprised and ashamed that my body obsessions didn't lessen or simply disappear while I was caring for Ronan; how guilty I felt that I couldn't shake that worry, that self-consciousness. It felt like a silly and fruitless obsession when I was losing my child: it was. It was also a lot easier to obsess about how my jeans fit than how I was going to bear the moment of his death or the life that came beyond it, and so in a way it was a wise coping mechanism.

The tricky territory of the body—how to work with it (which I interpreted as how to change or alter it), how to present it, how to live with it—was one I'd been trekking all my life, and so landing there felt familiar, driven by slightly self-destructive impulses that brought with them a recognizable and numbing solace. "Nobody needs to work out for three hours every day," my friends reminded me. "That's nutballs." Maybe. But what if it sometimes took me outside extreme feeling, and at other times emboldened me to go more deeply inside? Was it wearing me down, as people suggested, or helping me survive? I wasn't sure. I'm still not.

All of us in the body shit group felt bad about what we considered a "waste of time and energy." We all blamed ourselves. We all mentioned guilt. We were all certain that our bodies had gotten it wrong, were still getting it wrong, were still looking and acting all wrong.

What I've come to understand is that the way we feel about our bodies—whatever way that is—is not a waste of time and energy, and never fits into easy categories about what constitutes a "healthy body image." I can hear an early therapist of mine asking in a flat tone, her pen poised over her legal pad, "On a scale of one to ten, how would you rate your feelings about your body? As an example, 25 percent of respondents had ambivalent feelings." My response— "violent"—I could see clearly, from the therapist's pinched reaction, was the wrong one. Yet it seems ridiculous to say that there exist any graphs or pie charts or workbooks or weird quizzes that adequately sort out the terrors and memories of the body that are lived in its membranes and marrow, all of which are unique to each individual, and all of which are forged in the fire of our experiences. I wish I could say to that therapist and others I have known: I'm never going to fully accept my body, or think it's perfect *as it is,* but that doesn't mean I can't be happy and go through my day and experience joy and meaningful moments. I'm never going to fully accept that my son is gone, but that doesn't mean I can't be happy. Stop trying to fix my body shit and just let me figure out how to live with it.

If many of us feel anxious or uncomfortable with our appearance, and if grief is, as I believe, lived in and out of and through the body, then of course there is no magic trick to make these issues disappear; in fact, they may intensify. Shame, it seems, is a close cousin of grief, and I can trace mine back to some of its earliest origins, like following a labyrinth's circular path directly to the bull's-eye center, from which I can walk right back out again. I know it's there, but the path in and out never changes. I always take the same route. It might be hurtful, but at least I know what to expect.

In 1989, when I was fifteen years old, I bought a dress from the J. Crew catalog using the money I made working at the call-in catalog order center for the outdoor gear company Cabela's. There I earned a handful of dollars during each shift placing orders for camouflage pants, canteens, parkas, tents, and the occasional "deer drag" with its memorable sales pitch: "the best way to drag your kill from the forest intact." I was what my father described as a "violent vegetarian," so I wasn't keen on selling hunting supplies, but the call center was in our dumpy town; I could make the script sound "peppy" with my "pleasant phone voice," according to my creepy supervisor; and I needed the money: for a cheap car; for trips to Maurices at the mall; for college, which I hoped would be in New York City but which ended up being in Minnesota by parental decree.

My dress arrived in a plastic mailer, which felt fancy and special. "Delivery for you!" my dad shouted, and tossed the package up the stairs, where for nearly a week I'd been expectantly waiting on the landing around three o'clock in the afternoon, when the mail was delivered. I opened the mailer, and tucked inside a few sheets of carefully folded tissue paper, was a cotton mock turtleneck dress that fell to midcalf in a dark green color that matched my eyes. It cost fifty dollars, more than I'd ever spent on anything.

The fabric smelled new and clean; I imagined someone applying fresh green paint on the supersoft fabric. I slipped the dress over my head, my heart beating wildly. For someone who never showed her body, or at least not the lower half (which I also deliberately avoided looking at in mirrors), I was excited about how I looked from the waist up. The dress hid everything I wanted to hide, and emphasized everything I wanted to show. At the time, this felt like winning.

The next morning, I wound Clairol Hot Sticks into my hair to make tight ringlets, mimicking the perm my mother refused to let me have, applied Jean Naté body splash to my neck, and powder-puffed my face with Maybelline shimmer powder. I was feeling fine; I had noticed that boys— particularly one boy in chemistry class—had taken note of my new curves. This intrigued and confused and even frightened me, but the green dress made me feel bold and proud and attractive in a new way that was directly linked to independence: I had chosen it and paid for it with my own money.

As I walked down the stairs to grab my breakfast of a Snickers bar and a Diet Pepsi to consume in the car while my older brother drove me to school, the two of us speaking in our sibling language of grunts and nods, my grandmother passed through the hallway at the foot of the stairs. I stopped, expecting a compliment. She looked me up and down, made a dismissive *phhht* sound, and said, "Well, it sure is a good thing you're smart."

I skipped breakfast that day, and most meals for the next four years. When I graduated from high school, I weighed ninety-three pounds, and that green dress hung heavily from my shoulders, so oversized I looked like I was wearing a bag. I tried to forget about my body, and the forced forgetting consumed me. "The way to keep something is to forget it/Then it goes to an enormous place" (Jenny George, "Mnemonic"). That enormous place was my denial of what would fuel me, serve me; the strange logic of anorexia, thinking that if you could diminish the body, you could live without thinking about it.

My grandmother is dead now, and I understand that she was battling her own demons without any support, and that she was the most unkind to those she wanted most to love. The day of her January funeral at the family plot in central Illinois was so frigidly cold that it was almost impossible to break ground for her casket, which seemed to me an accurate visual for the way she loved, or didn't love, or perhaps just didn't know how to make a choice about how to love because she had no role models in her cruel and distant parents, mismatched German immigrants who shouted at each other and drank too much and never told her a thing about her body or what it might mean to be a woman in the world. I'm no longer anorexic, having moved past that stage in my twenties. But the impact of my grandmother's early comment—meant to wound, meant to land—on my body image and bedrock sense of self and worth is a wall I'm still working to knock down.

Enter: exercise.

When I learned to ski as a child through Winter Park's Adaptive Ski Program in Colorado, I felt freedom in the body for the first time, unencumbered by the awkward mechanics of a prosthesis, and buoyed by my coach, Hal, who was the kindest and toughest person I'd ever known. As a teenager in the 1980s I attended aerobics classes with my mother, with whom I did hundreds of leg lifts in the living room, first to cassette tapes (I vividly remember the stretch routine to the song "Bette Davis Eyes"—fingertips, knuckles, palm down, stand up!—which we played on the small pink "boom box" I received for my fourteenth birthday), and then to Jane Fonda tapes we found at garage sales. In college I stacked books inside crates, crafting a pseudo-step bench so I could keep working out to the Cher video I had done religiously nearly every day of senior year in high school. Step up, step down, jump up, jump down, I was sweating and huffing as the sun set through the frozen windows of my Minnesota dorm room, Cher's tiny body clad in black fishnets and a black leather leotard, the Eurythmics belting out the lyrics to "Missionary Man."

All of these exercises I so dutifully engaged with as an adult appealed to me because they promised, first and foremost, weight loss, which would, I imagined, lead to "transformation," that everyday wish that I mistook as analogous to my early sense of freedom as a skier. Exercise was also a complement to the countless diets I was always secretly on as a way to stay self-disciplined like my mother, who was a member of an organization that met once a week at our church called DDD (Diet, Discipline, and Discipleship). A red magnet shaped like an apple on our refrigerator read, NOTHING TASTES AS GOOD AS BEING THIN FEELS. I believed it.

Throughout my life, exercise has promised both release in the moment and a payoff beyond the moment that I hoped would make me feel better. As if losing yet another five pounds would help me ace a test, or write a killer essay, or, when Ronan was diagnosed, sit in the emotional tornado of rage and gutting sadness that I walked around in for two years, enveloping anyone who dared to get close.

During those two years of Ronan's illness, I ran on the

treadmill in a gray domed building where I also angrily pounded out the steps to Zumba routines, did sit-ups until my abdominal muscles trembled and cramped, lifted the heaviest weights I could find, trying to discover the quickest and most deliberate path to *hurt*. I hiked up the steepest mountains on sweltering and cold days, did hot yoga classes, back-to-back (so much sweat it was possible to cry without anyone knowing) until my clothes could be wrung out like soaked towels. At some point a friend of a friend bought me a heavy bag that I punched in the back room of my sunny rented house in Santa Fe until my arms were numb and the muscles popped.

Ronan was often with me at home, propped up in his high chair, sleeping, occasionally moving a fingertip, maybe a toe. I looked at him and punched and wept and then sat on the floor, wrapped my arms around the high chair and wept, until I was too tired to continue. I found an elliptical trainer for five hundred dollars on Craigslist and often used it for two hours at a time, moving my body to keep from moving it off a cliff, off a roof, into a first or second or third bottle of wine. These tactics were familiar: beating myself up under the guise of being "athletic." This behavior was further complicated by the fact that, as a person with a disability, I was applauded for being so "strong" and so "brave" to be engaging in any physical activity at all. The more sporty I was, the more I challenged perceptions of what it meant to be disabled, the more praise I received, and so I did more. But this time the praise didn't land or stick or provide even the tiniest moment of comfort. All I was left with was my grief, not diminished or subdued in the slightest, but hot and roiling and present in my skin, my eyeballs, my toes, my mouth, my belly. I still hated my body: for its asymmetry, for the fact that I had given birth to a child unable to live in the world, for all the ways my body was, as my aunt once announced to a room full of people, "made wrong." How could exercise help me now?

None of this shifted until my grief did, which is not to say that it lessened, only that it changed shape. After Charlie was born and Kent and I moved back to California, he bought me a gift for my forty-third birthday: a Peloton spin bike. In the basement, attached to a television, a rider has access to thousands of live and on-demand rides. The instructor is right there with you, you are face-to-face with them as they coach and encourage. On the first day I used it, I scrolled through the list of instructors, and landed on a face that looked open and pretty and badass: Christine. I signed into her class, choosing (of course) the hardest one I could find according to the ratings of previous riders. What was exercise if not pushing, if not punishment or penance?

It was *really challenging*. In fact, that was an actual zone of effort that Christine identified, just a step beneath *everything you've got*. At this point I'd been spinning for years, but not like this. Every class was coached; there was no sitting back and taking off all the resistance for a few minutes between songs; the effort was continuous, relentless. Christine's instructions, too, spoke to me: "What if you had to?" I remembered my friend Rachel walking through the door the day of Ronan's memorial, giving me a hug, and when she pulled back she looked me right in the eyes and said, "You did it." I thought of how people reacted when I told them I was pregnant with Charlie. "I couldn't do that if I were you. I'd be so afraid. You're so strong." All of this was running through my head, and I responded to those people in my imagination, saying, *I had a chance to be happy again*, and as my heart rate climbed higher and higher and I was panting and heaving and thinking and thinking, *Okay, I don't want to do this, this is too hard,* Christine said, "What if you had to?" And I thought of Ronan's face and the fact of Charlie and the unfairness and beauty of everything at once and I went faster and stronger than I ever had before, then collapsed in a puddle of tears, yelling up through the ceiling to Kent, "I fucking love this bike, thank you so much for getting it for me!"

As we were cooling down from that first ride, Christine said something else that resonated: that being in an uncomfortable place and staying in it makes a person proud. That was it: I was proud. Not of the way I looked, but proud for having endured. I could acknowledge that I had done what living beings are designed to do: fight to live. I could be proud of the way I had loved and continue to love my son without limits. I could be proud that I witnessed his first moment and his last. So much in the years with Tay-Sachs is unspeakable in its way. I gave everything I had; I went all the way to that final zone of effort and then beyond it. I was proud of opening up to love with Kent, impressed by my capacity to trust. I was proud of my choice to try to be a mother again, and I was proud of my daughter. I was proud that I had built a happy life against all the reasonable odds. What was I actually thinking? *I was proud of my body.* Maybe for the first time, ever, in my life. And what I felt in my body was a great release, and a new knowledge: this survival didn't make me special, as I'd been told as a young disabled girl; the work of it didn't transform me, as I had hoped it would when I was eating no more than eight hundred calories a day; instead, my living on after a great tragedy made me human. It was a fact. It just *was*.

I collapsed over the bike in a wave of grief and gratitude, and I've been taking Christine's classes ever since (and recruiting her to do grief retreats!), even the ones where we are *not pushing*, but recovering, which was a concept that finally resonated with me: the concept of self-care as pushing to no deadline, but just being in the breath. This invitation: to go through a physiological process mindfully, without judgment, with a scientific spirit of curiosity and discovery, reminds me also of what writing is about, what all creation is about.

There's a famous line about grief that "the only way out is through," but I think it's more accurate to say that the only way out is by going in, and then out again, then back in. Far, far in: to memory, to the breath, to the way you experience your beating heart in a burst of effort that you *choose*. Sometimes making a choice feels like a small liberation, even if it's the wrong one. And maybe you repeat this process again and again, and maybe it's just the motion that helps you live, and you don't have to learn any particular thing or process in any particular way. You just have to be *in it*.

In every book or essay or book review I have ever written, when faced with a narrative problem I cannot solve (or am likely avoiding), I used to write, "note to my smarter self to fix this" as a bolded instruction. What I've come to understand, however, is that there is no smarter self. There is only the self that lives and moves in the body, which has become a tool I never thought to utilize, even to respect, even to *like*. I've also learned that my grandmother was half-right: it's a good thing that the *body* is so smart; and forgiving, and, yes, resilient.

CHAPTER EIGHTEEN

On Beginnings and Shape-Shifting

The Trickster's paradoxical nature, combining two opposing as-
pects, often makes him a *threshold* deity—a god, if you will, of
transitional space. This was true, for example, of the archaic
Roman god Janus, whose names means "door" and who, by facing both ways, was the god of all gateways and passageways . . . as
patron of all entrances, he is also the protector and promoter of
all *beginnings*—hence also our January, the beginning of the
year. But he is also the god of exits, celebrated at the year's har-
vest, and early cults in his name worshipped Mars, god of war. In
the Roman Forum, his temple had two sets of swinging doors.
When the doors were closed, Rome was at peace. When the doors
were open, there was civil war. So Janus, like all Tricksters, em-
braces a pair of opposites.

DONALD KALSCHED, FROM *THE INNER WORLD OF TRAUMA:
ARCHETYPAL DEFENSES OF THE PERSONAL SPIRIT*

After Charlie was born, people asked me if I felt I had
replaced Ronan the way they thought I had replaced
one sad life with a happy one. As if people or relationships
are pieces on a board in some weird game of life checkers or
grief chess. A ridiculous idea, but not uncommon, I discovered; I realized that this notion, too, is linked to our faulty

conception of resilience. What I wanted to tell these well-meaning people was this: When Ronan was eighteen months old, exactly nine months after his diagnosis, he was strapped into a special therapy suit called a Thera-Tog—strips of bendable fabric that held him together, like the pieces of a pattern. Then, for a single bright and staggering moment, for the first and only time, he stood on his own feet. The wonder that crossed his face was for me, his mother, both remarkable and wrenching, as I knew it was possibly the only moment of joy he would ever have in his body. I would never know how he felt about it, because he would never have the ability to tell me. Watching Charlie, at the same age, stand with ease, and then run, and then talk, and then climb over rocks and waterfalls and chase butterflies and swim, her presence does not replace or erase his, but only evokes his absence more deeply, and often makes me feel guilty, or strange, or unworthy, or simply as if I'm floating above my own unreal life. Redefining resilience—seeing it anew—has helped me make sense of my life, which brings with it an uneasy peace that is better, at least, than a raging confusion.

What a great relief to understand, or to work to believe, as was the case with me, that resilience isn't a matter of flying over the mountain of grief into a new life; in fact, there is no willful action at all. Instead, a person dwells in the doorway, holding both lives, one on either side, trembling with grief and gratitude. Riding the rails, as it were, as I once did as a teenager.

We are all of us tricksters. It's how we live.

When Charlie is four, I take her with me to London to visit Emily. The two of them pretend to drive the double-decker bus from the top deck. I remember Emily sitting at the big wooden table in the church sanctuary, eating soup just a few weeks after Ronan died. We smoked cigarettes at the table and I had no appetite. I remember the first time I met her, the blue hat that matched her blue eyes, she was so rain-soaked she left puddles in her wake as she crossed the pub, waving and smiling at me as if she recognized me.

I sit behind Emily and Charlie as the bus rattles and twists through the lit, rain-slicked streets of London, marveling. Em's curly brown hair spins ringlets around the edge of her hat. Charlie refuses to let anyone brush her hair, so it sits in a messy topknot, the bleached ends like a white feather balanced at the top. "Go right! Don't hit that guy on the bike!" Charlie shouts, and she and Emily pretend to struggle to turn the pretend steering wheel they both pretend to share. Charlie is so *alive*, but she is not in Ronan's place, not a "replacement child." Instead, she is living her life alongside him, if you count memory as a living thing. Maybe he's the cyclist who grabs the edge of the bus to get a bit of speed going around the corner. Maybe he's the boy we pass waiting in the bus shelter, rain waterfalling around him.

One dead child. One living child. These simple facts are full of mysteries so wholly complicated and complex that the smartest scientists have not yet found a way to unravel them. We know about dark matter, but we don't know how to see it, to detect it, to *prove* it. The work of resilience is to embrace the opposites; to be the trickster; to dwell in that middle place, in the moment between the doors swinging open and then swinging shut. James Baldwin wrote: "Any real change implies the breakup of the world as one has always known it, the loss of all that gave one an identity, the end of safety."

Loss of identity is not loss of life. We don't always need to know who we are or why things end in order to live; sometimes it might be more bearable if we don't. Hope, like the study of dark matter, is always about proving the unseen, and often the not yet known.

Threshold

At the end of my suffering
there was a door.

Hear me out: that which you call death
I remember.

Overhead, noises, branches of the pine shifting.
Then nothing. The weak sun
flickered over the dry surface.

It is terrible to survive
as consciousness
buried in the dark earth.

Then it was over: that which you fear, being
a soul and unable
to speak, ending abruptly, the stiff earth
bending a little. And what I took to be
birds darting in low shrubs.

You who do not remember
passage from the other world
I tell you I could speak again: whatever
returns from oblivion returns
to find a voice:

from the center of my life came
a great fountain, deep blue
shadows on azure seawater.

LOUISE GLÜCK, "THE WILD IRIS"

At the end of my suffering/there was a door." I read this line from Louise Glück's poem "The Wild Iris" in 2001, when I was twenty-seven years old. On one mild Texas winter day I sat reading on a swing at the top of a small hill overlooking a muddy patch of the Guadalupe River. I thought I was living a romantic writerly dream in Martindale, a small, dusty town of a few hundred residents south of Austin, but in truth, I hated it. The air drooped with bugs, no matter the season or hour of the day. Cockroaches scattered each time I opened the screen door and often perched, like burglars caught in the act—on the shower curtain, on my desk, in a stack of dirty dishes.

In the summer, drunken river revelers floated by on inner tubes and threw their empty beer cans on the lawn that sloped down to the murky water's edge. The swaying trees in the yard offered shade but no relief from the heat, which felt like a heavy hand pressing down on the top of my head. An abandoned schoolhouse surrounded by a chain-link fence faced the house, guarding the other side of the gravel road, and farther along on that same street (which was Main Street), a man who wore overalls and no shirt tinkered with rotting cars in a tumbledown brick building, a faded American flag stretched across one wall, end to end. Each time I ran past him he said, as if for the first time, "If it hurts so much to run, why don't you just walk? It pains me to watch you." Each time I waved without smiling, and kept running (more of a limp-run, but I was consistent at least).

When I ran at night, which I often did just to avoid this awkward interaction, and because I was embarrassed by my strange and painful-looking running gait, the light from the snapping streetlights made bone-like shadows around the cars' wrecked bodies. In the flickering light these skeletons appeared to rise in order to take off in a gutted Mustang or a boat-sized Plymouth. Each night, every night, and all night, the pit bull tethered to a post in front of the house across the road wailed and howled and growled and barked, straining against the thick chain, biting the air, gums gleaming, his tail wildly sweeping back and forth, as if this might somehow loosen him from his cruel captivity. He'd been trapped there so long that the collar had grown into the flesh of his neck. I wondered if freeing him might kill him.

As a graduate student, when I wasn't running or writing or thinking about writing, I was reading. I had always taken refuge in the life of the mind, and now I wanted to be a writer. Navigating emotional territory through the written word would become my specialty. I was earnest, but also anxious. "Writing takes a remarkable resilience of spirit," my favorite writing teacher had promised, or perhaps it was a warning. Did I have this quality? I looked for the answer in poetry, novels, memoirs, and essays. I never thought to look closely at the wider world and the objects and creatures within it for lessons about how to live and love. I never thought about the staying power of *things* in the world, and what could be learned from the great materiality and texture and mystery of objects and phenomena, known or unknown, and their power to impart meaning across time solely by virtue of their existence. I never thought about what the events of my own life examined *within* and as parts of the context of that world might teach me, how the world itself might hold me, even when I felt it had betrayed me. How its dynamism and its passivity might open a door to possibility. Instead, I was trapped inside my own thoughts. A lot.

On that particular overcast afternoon, Glück's line knocked me out of my delusions—of grandeur or intelligence—as I sensed a truth in it that was both familiar and strange. It was a genius line, of course, and I desperately wanted to be a genius, but it was more than that. It was something more fundamental—the bottom of a feeling that grows up into emotion, either forcefully, through trauma, or thoughtfully, through attentive care. I couldn't think my way into it, which frustrated and moved me. This line did not require my intelligence; it required my full presence, which I was (and always had been) reluctant to give. I knew I was reading a truth I did not yet know and I felt a sharp point of pressure behind each of my eyes. I was softened, alert, and also guided in some way. How would I uncover that nugget, whole, and hold it in my hands? Was I equipped to deal with it if I managed to work it free? To what or whom would it belong? What were the responsibilities of being the guardian of this truth, or was guarding any kind of truth a distinct impossibility, just another inflation of the ego, another act of hubris? The pain and triumph expressed in that single line were beyond my capacity, although I did not yet know how, or why, and this frightened me.

An old graveyard formed the ragged boundary of the backyard that sloped to the river. I often visited this tree-shaded square, the size of a small park, feeling the gentle pull of mud against my feet as I walked through the uneven rows of gravestones. Robert Hass's observation in *Twentieth Century Pleasures: Prose on Poetry* that "the whole difference between the nineteenth century and the twentieth century could be summed up in two words, graveyard and cemetery" resonated with me. This was certainly a graveyard, and the stones marked the resting places of Confederate soldiers, but most marked the graves of babies and children: two months old, two days old, four years old, six weeks old, five and fifteen. Thomas, John, Robert, James. Edith, Mary, Anne. Solid names. A low, almost cool-ish fog—thin as a vapor—that would burn off when the sun began its daily blaze was slung like a thin canopy over the untended graves. Nineteen sixty-five was the most recent death date I could find, although I searched, as if a newer headstone might reveal some fresh truth that the older ones could no longer provide. I brushed back weeds as tall as I was as I made my way into the older section, some of the stones leaning there to the left or right, haphazard as if they'd been tossed, like those I would one day see at Jerusalem's Mount of Olives, a hillside dotted with gravestones that seemed loosened from the earth, like rotting teeth about to fall from a diseased mouth.

I lingered over the baby graves—aghast, saddened, subdued. I half expected to see the graves of the parents right beside those of their children, separated only by a matter of months, days, minutes. *What did those parents do?* I wondered. *Where did they go?* I could stay in this somber, melodramatic mode of questioning because I had never had a child. If I had, I would have turned, wordlessly, walked away from the graveyard and never returned.

"At the end of my suffering/there was a door"—it took me thirteen years, two marriages, two children, two homes, two deserts—in truth, two *lives*—to understand this line, and to make peace with its terms, which have been brutal, but also blazing and necessary.

We think the solution is obvious: a griever survives to walk through to another space, the other side, closing the door on an experience gratefully left behind; this is how I initially understood Glück's line. The suffering was over. *Slam.* And now a new life, a bright and shining salvation, uncomplicated and complete. A resurrection. "Jesus is *risen*," people chant on Easter Sunday. He doesn't linger in the doorway or loiter in some liminal space between heaven and earth. He's gone. To find him you must look up and you must believe. But none of us lives in the Bible, and I don't believe in resurrections or in any God.

This is what it was, and this is what I believe: There was great suffering. Then there was a door. I stood in the threshold of that door and understood that I would always be there, at the opening, sometimes clinging to the hinges. Just as the door opened to love, it would remain wide open to suffering. This is the only way to live, and the only way to love in the manner that I had always wanted to love without knowing what it felt like, or what it might cost me. Then the whole world became my teacher. Those are the terms Glück's line crystallizes, the terms it took me one quarter of my life to understand and accept, although on some days I still want to reject them.

One early morning when I was out for a run on my usual route, I saw that the dog across the street had finally broken free of his stake, although it was still attached to him, as was the rusted, rattling chain. Surprised, I stopped, almost falling over my feet, feeling the artificial knee freeze up, swallowing each heartbeat and wishing for once that my mechanic friend would make an appearance at this predawn hour and help me out in case this encounter took an ugly turn. The dog stood in the middle of the road, his skinny black body trembling, his ribs a visible cage around which his ragged, filthy fur alive with fleas was stretched. He growled once, a distinct warning. Sweat blurred my vision, but I didn't swipe at my eyes or move at all for fear this would be interpreted as aggression. We stood facing each other for a few moments, motionless as if under a spell, although I could see the dog was shaking as I was. I fought to catch my breath. The dog, teeth bared, fought to keep still. Finally he turned and ran down the road, the chain rattling behind him, a snake of dust curling up in his wake.

The dog disappeared around the corner, the dust settled, and all that was left to see was that open road, the flat land stretching into the hazy distance, and the red-gold sun popping up on the horizon. Sweaty and still, I stood in awe of him, for running with and through his fear, running no matter what, running because he could. I could no longer see him but I imagined him: broken and trembling and terrified and damaged, he was still headed somewhere, resilient not because he left his difficult life behind for something better, but because, like all of us, he carried the source and the history of his pain with him. The instruments of his suffering were also part of his survival.

This, then, is how we all must—and do—live.

ACKNOWLEDGMENTS

All writing is, at its core, an act of collaboration. Writers create nothing alone; they rely on others for guidance, support, and editorial genius. This is particularly true for me as I work alongside my mind soulmate, the unparalleled editor, Andrea Walker, and my beloved, together-for-life agent, Dorian Karchmar, who together help me shape my vision and examine every word and idea and misstep under a magnifying glass. My forever dream team, you two. Every single day I am thankful for you both, and for all that you have made possible for me. Thank you, Emma Caruso and Alex Kane, who have to wrangle paperwork out of me and are charged with keeping me organized. You are deeply appreciated, as are all the people at WME and Penguin Random House who make books and stories continue to matter when we need them most.

Thank you to my parents, Mary and Roger, for sharing their stories here, and for being my allies at every dramatic, triumphant, and wrenching stage of my life. They witnessed my birth, the birth and death of my son, and the birth of my daughter, and every moment in between. I am indebted to their grace and kindness; and I am grateful that they offered, through the narratives of their own lives, early case studies in resilience. Thank you, John Edward Gorman and Lorene Slagell Gorman, alive only in my grief city. Thank you, Kate, Kristen, and Kerry, for being the "cousins." Thank you, James Lynch, for everything: Let's always get those shoes.

Thank you to my many beloved friends, whom I love: you know who you are. Without your love and laughter and honesty and support and sparkle, life would not have its texture or taste or fun. Thanks to my astro-twin Lisa Glatt, my partner in so many necessary literary adventures. Thank you, Carrie Scanga, who always makes visual the deepest parts of my heart in the most amazing way; I love collaborating with you. Thank you, Katie Ford, genius poet, who read every line of this book, and who has been writing poems that track straight lines to my heart for two decades. Thank you, Annemarie Hauser, "older daughter" and quarantine queen, who at this moment is wrangling the cat out of the grocery bags that arrived from Instacart during the Covid-19 epidemic and who is so dear and beloved to me. Thank you, Emily Miles, for being the person who knows me best. Thank you, Barbara Pitkin, for your mentorship. Thank you, Gina Frangello, for the world's best (and longest!) text messages.

Thank you, Weber, for always showing up. Thank you, LC, for your ponderous, faithful presence: "Manana Forever." Thank you, Sarah Sentilles, love warrior. Thank you, Angela Giles, for "wings of truth." Thank you, Julie Coyne, for modeling true compassion. Thank you, Monika Bustamante and Chris Simpson, for your long-term and steadfast friendship. Thank you, Lucy Kalanithi, for sisterhood. Thank you, Cynthia and Yaron, for a home in NYC. Thank you, Nancy and Libby, for embodying the true meaning of hospitality. Thank you, Tara Ison and Bernadette Murphy, guides. Thank you, Elizabeth Silver, for reading an early, messy draft.

Thank you to my colleagues at the University of California-Riverside, and at the University of California-Palm Desert. I am fortunate and grateful to have these people in my orbit. Tod Goldberg, thank you for making me laugh. David L. Ulin, thank you. Elizabeth Crane, Rob Roberge, John Schimmel, and Mark Haskell Smith, thank you. Agam Patel, a million thank yous. Thank you, Alison Benis White for "murder yoga." Thank you, Andrew Winer and Tom Lutz, for having my back. Thank you, Bryan Bradford. Thank you to all of my students, who continue to inspire and challenge me, especially Calista Fernandez and Serena Trujillo, rock stars and the future of literature. You give me so much hope. Thank you to all the writers I work with who have trusted me with their stories.

Thank you, Christine D'Ercole and the entire Peloton community, for the power of discipline and sweat. Thank you, Joni Green, for making me strong. Thank you to Rebecca Soffer, Casa Soffer, and the Modern Loss community, for making grief livable. Thank you, Juliana Jones-Munson, for shutting down the circus. Thank you, Ohayon family: Margaret, Jonathan, Maeille, Kaeli, and Aeden, for being my friendship rocks in the stream, and for celebrating all the Jewish holidays with me. Thank you to Jenny and Lexi, to Monica and Tiara and Kara, for teaching my child, even when the world was closed down. Thank you, KC and Natalie, Desiree, Alisa and Ryan, my parent friends.

Thank you to my "Loss Ladies": Lorie Adair, Michaela Evanow, Amy Fleury, Becky Benson, Esther Levy, Kate Suddes, and Penne Richards. I hope we will keep writing and talking about our children forever.

To Ronan, my lost boy: I miss you, I love you, and I visit you every day in the city of grief.

Thank you to Kent Black, loving father and good man, for giving me the gift of our wonderful, incandescent, spunky, gorgeous, kind, funny, smart, adventurous, generous, bright sprite light of a ginger girl, Charlotte Mabel Elliott Black. This book would not exist without you.

And finally, to Charlie Girl, if and when you read this story: I hope you will know and understand that any crucible was worth moving through to find the sanctuary of being your mother. I love you completely and forever and with all my heart. You are my favorite person, now and forever.

EMILY RAPP BLACK is the author of *Poster Child: A Memoir* and *The Still Point of the Turning World*. A onetime Fulbright scholar, she was educated at Harvard University, Trinity College Dublin, Saint Olaf College, and the University of Texas at Austin, where she was a James A. Michener fellow. A recent Guggenheim Fellowship recipient, she has received awards and fellowships from the Rona Jaffe Foundation, Jentel Arts, Yaddo, the Fine Arts Work Center in Provincetown, Fundación Valparaíso, and Bucknell University's Philip Roth Residency in Creative Writing. Her work has appeared in *Vogue, The New York Times, Salon, Slate, Time, The Boston Globe, The Wall Street Journal, Psychology Today, O: The Oprah Magazine, Los Angeles Times,* and many others. She is a regular contributor to *The New York Times Book Review* and frequently publishes scholarly work in the fields of disability studies, bioethics, and theological studies. She is currently associate professor of creative writing at the University of California, Riverside, where she also teaches medical narratives in the School of Medicine.

emilyrappblack.com
Twitter: @emilyrappblack1
Instagram: @emilyrappblack